SECRET ARMIES

SECRET ARMIES

THE NEW TECHNIQUE OF NAZI WARFARE

John L. Spivak

MAPLE SPRING PUBLISHING

Published 2025 by Maple Spring Publishing

Interior design by Jason Snyder
Cover design by Tom McKeveny

Library of Congress Cataloging-in-Publication Data is available upon request

ISBN: 979-8-3505-0169-8

10   9   8   7   6   5   4   3   2   1

CONTENTS

PREFACE

THE MATERIAL IN THIS SMALL VOLUME just barely scratches the surface of a problem which is becoming increasingly grave: the activities of Nazi agents in the United States, Mexico, and Central America. During the past five years I have observed some of them, watching the original, crudely organized and directed propaganda machine develop, grow and leave an influence far wider than most people seem to realize. What at first appeared to be merely a distasteful attempt by Nazi Government officials at direct interference in the affairs of the American people and their Government, has now assumed the more sinister aspect of also seeking American naval and military secrets.

Further studies in Central America, Mexico and the Panama Canal Zone disclosed an espionage network directed by the Rome-Berlin-Tokyo axis and operating against the peace and security of the United States. A scrutiny of the Nazi Fifth Column[1] in a few European countries, especially in Czechoslovakia just before that Republic was turned

1 When the Spanish Insurgents were investing Madrid early in November, 1936, newspaper correspondents asked Insurgent General Emilio Mola which of his four columns would take the city. Mola replied enigmatically: "The Fifth Column." He referred to the fascist sympathizers within Madrid—those attempting to abet the defeat of the Spanish Government by means of spying, sabotage and terrorism. The term "Fifth Column" is today widely used to describe the various fascist and Nazi organizations operating within the borders of non-fascist nations.

over to Germany's mercy by the Munich "peace" and in France where Nazi and Italian agents built an amazing secret underground army, has made the fascist activities in the Western Hemisphere somewhat clearer to me.

I have included one chapter detailing events which cannot, so far as I have been able to discover, be traced directly to Nazi espionage; but it shows the influence of Nazi ideology upon England's now notorious "Cliveden set," which maneuvered the betrayal of Austria, sacrificed Czechoslovakia and is working in devious ways to strengthen Hitler in Europe. The "Cliveden set" has already had so profound an effect upon the growth and influence of fascism throughout the world, that I thought it advisable to include it.

The sources for most of the material, by its very nature, naturally cannot be revealed. Those conversations which I quote directly came from people who were present when they occurred or, as in the case of the Cagoulards in France, from official records. In the chapter on Czechoslovakia I quote a conversation between a Nazi spy and his chief. The details came to me from a source which in the past I had found accurate. Subsequently, the spy was arrested by Czech secret police, and his confession substantiated the conversation as I have given it.

Much of the material in this volume has been published in various periodicals from time to time, but so many Americans feel that concern over Nazi penetration in this country is exaggerated, that I hope even this brief and incomplete picture will serve to impress the reader, as it has impressed me, with the gravity of the situation.

J. L. S.

I CZECHOSLOVAKIA— BEFORE THE CARVING

IT IS PRETTY GENERALLY ADMITTED now that the Munich "peace" gave Germany industrial and military areas essential to further aggressions. Instead of helping to put a troubled Europe on the road to lasting peace, Munich strengthened the totalitarian powers, especially Germany, and a strengthened Germany inevitably means increased activities of the Nazis' Fifth Column which is, in all quarters of the globe, actively preparing the ground for Hitler's greater plans.

If we can divine the future by the past, the Fifth Column, that shadowy group of secret agents now entrenched in every important country throughout the world, is an omen of what is to come. Before Germany marched into Austria, that unhappy country witnessed a large influx of Fifth Column members. In Czechoslovakia, especially in those months before the Republic's heart was handed to Hitler on a platter, there was a tremendous increase in the numbers and activities of agents sent into the Central European country.

During my stay there in the brief period immediately preceding the "peace," I learned a little about the operations of the Gestapo's secret agents in Czechoslovakia. Their numbers are vast and those few of whom I learned, are infinitesimal to the actual numbers at work then and now, not only in Czechoslovakia but in other countries. What I learned of those few, however, shows how the Gestapo, the Nazi secret service, operates in its ruthless drive.

For years Hitler had laid plans to fight, if he had to, for Czechoslovakia, whose natural mountain barriers and man-made defensive line of steel and concrete stood in the way of his announced drive to the Ukrainian wheat fields. In preparation for the day when he might have to fight for its control, he sent into the Republic a host of spies, provocateurs, propagandists and saboteurs to establish themselves, make contacts, carry on propaganda and build a machine which would be invaluable in time of war.

In a few instances I learned the details of the Nazis' inexorable determination and their inhuman indifference to the lives of even their own agents.

※　※　※

Arno Oertel, *alias* Harald Half, was a thin, white-faced spy trained in two Gestapo schools for Fifth Column work. Oertel was given a German passport by Richter, the Gestapo district chief at Bischofswerda on what was then the Czechoslovak-German frontier.

"You will proceed to Prague," Richter instructed him, "and lose yourself in the city. As soon as it is safe, go to Langenau near Boehmisch-Leipa and report to Frau Anna Suchy.[2] She will give you further instructions."

Oertel nodded. It was his first important espionage job—assigned to him after the twenty-five-year-old secret agent had finished his intensive course in the special Gestapo training school in Zossen (Brandenburg), one of the many schools established by the Nazi secret service to train agents for various activities.

2 Frau Suchy was one of the most active members of Konrad Henlein's *Deutscher Volksbund,* a propaganda and espionage organization masquerading as a "cultural" body in the Sudeten area. She is today a leading official in the new German Sudetenland.

After his graduation Oertel had been given minor practical training in politically disruptive work in anti-fascist organizations across the Czech border where he had posed as a German emigré. There he had shown such aptitude that his Gestapo chief at sector headquarters in Dresden, Herr Geissler, sent him to Czechoslovakia on a special mission.

Oertel hesitated. "Naturally I'll take all possible precautions but— accidents may happen."

Richter nodded. "If you are caught and arrested, demand to see the German Consul immediately," he said. "If you are in a bad predicament, we'll request your extradition on a criminal charge—burglarly with arms, attempted murder—some non-political crime. We've got a treaty with Czechoslovakia to extradite Germans accused of criminal acts but—" The Gestapo chief opened the top drawer of his desk and took a small capsule from a box. "If you find yourself in an utterly hopeless situation, swallow this."

He handed the pellet to the nervous young man.

"Cyanide," Richter said. "Tie it up in a knot in your handkerchief. It will not be taken from you if you are arrested. There is always an opportunity while being searched to take it."

Oertel tied the pellet in a corner of his handkerchief and placed it in his breast pocket.

"You are to make two reports," Richter continued. "One for Frau Suchy, the other for the contact in Prague. She'll get you in touch with him."

Anna Suchy, when Oertel reported to her, gave him specific orders: "On August 16 [1937], at five o'clock in the afternoon, you will sit on a bench near the fountain in Karlsplatz in Prague. A man dressed in a gray suit, gray hat, with a blue handkerchief showing from the breast pocket of his coat, will ask you for a light for his cigarette. Give him the light and accept a cigarette from the gentleman. He will give you detailed instructions on what to do and how to meet the Prague contact to whom in turn you will report."

At the appointed hour Oertel sat on a bench staring at the fountain, watching men and women strolling and chatting cheerfully on the way to meet friends for late afternoon coffee. Occasionally he looked at the afternoon papers lying on the bench beside him. He felt that he was being watched but he saw no one in a gray suit with a blue handkerchief. He wiped his forehead with his handkerchief, partly because of the heat, partly because of nervousness. As he held the handkerchief he could feel the tightly bound capsule.

Precisely at five he noticed a man in a gray suit with a gray hat and a blue handkerchief in the breast pocket of his coat, strolling toward him. As the man approached he took out a package of cigarettes, selected one and searched his pockets for a light. Stopping before Oertel, he doffed his hat and smilingly asked for a light. Oertel produced his lighter and the other in turn offered him a cigarette. He sat down on the bench.

"Report once a week," he said abruptly, puffing at his cigarette and staring at two children playing in the sunshine which flooded Karlsplatz. He stretched his feet like a man relaxing after a hard day's work. "Deliver reports to Frau Suchy personally. One week she will come to Prague, the next you go to her. Deliver a copy of your report to the English missionary, Vicar Robert Smith, who lives at 31 Karlsplatz."

Smith, to whom the unidentified man in the gray suit told Oertel to report, was a minister of the Church of Scotland in Prague, a British subject with influential connections not only with English-speaking people but with Czech government officials.[3] Besides his ministerial

---

3 The Rev. Smith returned to England when he learned that the Czechoslovakian secret police were watching him. At the present writing he had not returned to his church in Prague.

work, the Reverend Smith led an amateur orchestra group giving free concerts for German emigrés. On his clerical recommendation, he got German "emigré" women into England as house servants for British government officials and army officers.

※　※　※

The far-flung Gestapo network in Czechoslovakia concentrated much of its activities along the former German-Czech border. In Prague, even today when Germany has achieved what she said was all she wanted in Europe, the network reaches into all branches of the Government, the military forces and emigré anti-fascist groups. The country, before it was cut to pieces and even now, is honeycombed with Gestapo agents sent from Germany with false passports or smuggled across the border.

Often the Gestapo uses Czech citizens whose relatives are in Germany and upon whom pressure is put. The work of these agents consists not only of ferreting out military information regarding Czech defense measures and establishing contacts with Czech citizens for permanent espionage, but of the equally important assignment of disrupting anti-fascist groups—of creating opposition within organizations having large memberships in order to split and disintegrate them. Agents also make reports on public opinion and attitudes, and record carefully the names and addresses of those engaged in anti-fascist work. A similar procedure was followed in Austria before that country was invaded, and it enabled the Nazis to make wholesale arrests immediately upon entering the country.

Prague, with a German population of sixty thousand is still the headquarters for the astonishing espionage and propaganda machine which the Gestapo built throughout the country. Before Czechoslovakia was cut up, most of the espionage reports crossed the frontier into Germany through Tetschen-Bodenbach. The propaganda and espionage center of the Henlein group was in the headquarters of the *Sudeten Deutsche Partei* at 4 Hybernska St. A secondary headquarters, in the *Deutscher Hilfsverein* at 7 Nekazanka St., was directed by Emil Wallner, who was ostensibly representing the Leipzig Fair but was actually the chief of the Gestapo machine in Prague. His assistant, Hermann Dorn, living in Hanspaulka-Dejvice, masqueraded as the representative of the *Muenchner Illustrierte Zeitung.*

Some aspects of the Nazi espionage and propaganda machine in Czechoslovakia hold especial interest for American immigration authorities since into the United States, too, comes a steady flow of the shadowy members of the Nazis' Fifth Column. It is well to know that the letters and numbers at the top of passports inform German diplomatic representatives the world over that the bearer usually is a Gestapo agent. Whenever American immigration authorities find German passports with letters and numbers at the top, they may be reasonably sure that the bearer is an agent. These numbers are placed on passports by Gestapo headquarters in Berlin or Dresden. The agent's photograph and a sample of his (or her) handwriting is sent via the diplomatic pouch to the Nazi Embassy, Legation, Consulate or German Bund in the country or city to which the agent is assigned. When the agent reports in a foreign city, the resident Gestapo chief, in order to identify him, checks the passport's top number with the picture and the handwriting received by diplomatic pouch.

⁂ ⁂ ⁂

Rudolf Walter Voigt, *alias* Walter Clas, *alias* Heinz Leonhard, *alias* Herbert Frank—names which he used throughout Europe in his espionage work will serve as an illustration. Voigt was sent to Prague on a delicate mission. His job was to discover how Czechs got to Spain to fight in the International Brigade, a mystery in Berlin since such Czechs had to cross Italy, Germany or other fascist countries which cooperate with the Gestapo.

Voigt was given passport No. 1,128,236 made out in the name of Walter Clas, and bearing at the top of the passport the letters and numbers 1A1444. He was instructed, by Leader Wilhelm May of Dresden, to report to the Henlein Party headquarters upon his arrival in Prague. Clas, *alias* Voigt, arrived October 23, 1937, reported at the Sudeten Party headquarters and saw a man whom I was unable to identify. He was instructed to report again four days later, since information about the agent had not yet arrived.

Voigt was trained in the Gestapo espionage schools in Potsdam and Calmuth-Remagen. He operates directly under Wilhelm May whose headquarters are in Dresden. May is in charge of Gestapo work over Sector No. 2. Preceding the granting to Hitler of the Sudeten areas in Czechoslovakia, the entire Czech border espionage and terrorist activity was divided into sectors. At this writing the same sector divisions still exist, operating now across the new frontiers. Sector No. 1 embraces Silesia with headquarters at Breslau; No. 2, Saxony, with headquarters at Dresden; and No. 3, Bavaria, with headquarters at Munich. After the annexation of Austria, Sector No. 4 was added, commanded by Gestapo Chief Scheffler whose headquarters are in Berlin with a branch in Vienna. Sector No. 4 also directs *Standarte II* which stands ready to provide incidents to justify German invasion "because the situation has got out of control of the local authorities."

Another way in which immigration authorities, especially in countries surrounding Germany, can detect Gestapo agents is by the position of stamps on the German passport. Stamps are placed, in accordance with German law, directly under the spot provided for them on the passport on the front page, upper right hand corner. Whenever the stamps are on the cover facing the passport title page, it is a sign to

Gestapo representatives and Consulates that the bearer is an agent who crossed the border hurriedly without time to get the regular numbers and letters from Gestapo headquarters. The agent is given this means of temporary identification by the border Gestapo chief.

Also, whenever immigration authorities find a German passport issued to the bearer for less than five years and then extended to the regulation five-year period, they may be certain that the bearer is a new Gestapo agent who is being tested by controlled movements in a foreign country. For his first Gestapo mission in Holland, for instance, Voigt was given a passport August 15, 1936, good for only fourteen days. His chief was not sure whether or not Voigt had agreed to become an agent just to get a passport and money to escape the country; so his passport period was limited.

When the fourteen-day period expired, Voigt would have to report to the Nazi Consulate for a renewal. In this particular instance, the passport was marked "Non-renewable Except by Special Permission of the Chief of Dresden Police." When Voigt performed his Holland mission successfully, he was given the usual five-year passport.

※　※　※

Any German whose passport shows a given limited time, which has been subsequently extended, gives proof that he has been tested and found satisfactory by the Gestapo.

II ENGLAND'S CLIVEDEN SET

THE WORK OF FOREIGN AGENTS does not necessarily involve the securing of military and naval secrets. Information of all kinds is important to an aggressor planning an invasion or estimating a potential enemy's strength and morale; and often a diplomatic secret is worth far more than the choicest blueprint of a carefully guarded military device.

There are persons whom money, social position, political promises or glory cannot interest in following a policy of benefit to a foreign power. In such instances, however, protection of class interests sometimes drives them to acts which can scarcely be distinguished from those of paid foreign agents. This is especially true of those whose financial interests are on an international scale and who consequently think internationally.

Such class interests were involved in the betrayal of Austria to the Nazis only a few months before aggressor nations were invited to cut themselves a slice of Czechoslovakia; and it will probably never be known just how much the Nazis' Fifth Column, working in dinner jackets and evening gowns, influenced the powerful personages involved to chart a course which sacrificed a nation and a people and which foretold the Munich "peace" pact.

The story begins when Neville Chamberlain, Prime Minister of England, accepted an invitation to spend the weekend of March 26-27,

1938, at Cliveden, Lord and Lady Astor's country estate at Taplow, Buckinghamshire, in the beautiful Thames Valley. When the Prime Minister and his wife arrived at the huge Georgian house rising out of a fairyland of gardens and forests with the placid river for a background, the other guests who had already arrived and their hosts were under the horseshoe stone staircase to receive them.

The small but carefully selected group of guests had been invited "to play charades" over the weekend—a game in which the participants form opposing sides and act a certain part while the opponents try to guess what they are portraying. Every man invited held a strategic position in the British government, and it was during this "charades party" weekend that they secretly charted a course of British policy which will affect not only the fate of the British Empire but the course of world events and the lives of countless millions of people for years to come.

This course, which indirectly menaces the peace and security of the United States, deliberately launched England on a series of maneuvers which made Hitler stronger and will inevitably lead Great Britain on the road to fascism. The British Parliament and the British people do not know of these decisions, some of which the Chamberlain government has already carried out.

And without a knowledge of what happened during the talks in those historic two days and what preceded them, the world can only puzzle over an almost incomprehensible British foreign policy.

Present at this weekend gathering, besides the Astors and the Prime Minister and his wife, were the following:

Sir Thomas Inskip, Minister for Defense.

Sir Alexander Cadogan, who replaced Sir Robert Vansittart as adviser to the British Cabinet and who acts in a supervisory capacity over the extraordinarily powerful British Intelligence Service.

Geoffrey Dawson, editor of the London *Times.*

Lord Lothian, Governor of the National Bank of Scotland, a determined advocate of refusing arms to the Spanish democratic government while Hitler and Mussolini supplied Franco with them.

Tom Jones, adviser to former Premier Baldwin.

The Right Honorable E. A. Fitzroy, Speaker of the House of Commons.

The Baroness Mary Ravensdale, sister-in-law of Sir Oswald Mosley, leader of the British fascist movement.

To understand the amazing game played by the Cliveden house guests, in which nations and peoples have already been shuffled about as pawns, one must remember that powerful German industrialists and financiers like the Krupps and the Thyssens supported Hitler primarily in order to crush the German trade-union and political movements which were in the late 1920s threatening their wealth and power.

The Astors are part of the same family in the United States. Lady Nancy Astor, born in Virginia, married into one of the richest families in England. Her interests and the interests of Viscount Astor, her husband, stretch into banking, railroads, life insurance and journalism. Half a dozen members of the family are in Parliament: Lady Astor, her husband, their son, in the House of Commons; and two relatives in the House of Lords. The Astor family controls two of the most powerful and influential newspapers in the world, the London *Times* and the London *Observer.* In the past these papers, whose influence cannot be exaggerated, have been strong enough to make and break Prime Ministers.

Cliveden House, ruled by the intensely energetic and ambitious American-born woman, had already left its mark upon current history following other weekend parties. Lady Astor and her coterie had been playing a more or less minor role in the affairs of the largest empire in the world, but decisions recently reached at her weekend parties have already changed the map of Europe, after almost incredible intrigues, betrayals and double-crossings, carried through with the ruthlessness of a conquering Caesar and the boundless ambitions of a Napoleon.

The weekends at Cliveden House which culminated in the historic one of March 26–27, began in the fall of 1937. Lady Astor had been having teas with Lady Ravensdale and had entertained von Ribbentrop, Nazi Ambassador to Great Britain, at her town house. Gradually the Astor-controlled London *Times* assumed a pro-Nazi bias on its very influential editorial page. When the *Times* wants to launch a campaign, its custom is to run a series of letters in its famous correspondence columns and then an editorial advocating the policy decided upon. During October, 1937, the *Times* sprouted letters regarding Hitler's claims for the return of the colonies taken from Germany after the war.

Rather than have Germany attack her, England preferred to see Hitler turn his eyes to the fertile Ukrainian wheat fields of the Soviet Union. It meant war, but that war seemed inevitable. If Russia won, England and her economic royalists would be faced with "the menace of communism." But if Germany won, she would expand eastward and, exhausted by the war, would be in no condition to make demands upon England. The part Great Britain's economic royalists had to play, then, was to strengthen Germany in her preparations for the coming war with Russia and at the same time prepare herself to fight if her calculations went wrong.

Cabinet ministers Lord Hailsham (sugar and insurance interests), Lord Swinton (railroads, power, with subsidiaries in Germany, Italy, etc.), Sir Samuel Hoare (real estate, insurance, etc.), were felt out and thought it was a good idea. Chamberlain himself had a hefty interest (around twelve thousand shares) in Imperial Chemical Industries, affiliated with *I. G. Farbenindustrie,* the German dye trust which is very actively supplying Hitler with war materials. The difficulty was Anthony Eden, British Foreign Minister, who was opposed to fascist aggressions because he feared they would eventually threaten the British Empire. Eden would certainly not approve of strengthening fascist countries and encouraging them to still greater aggressions.

At one of the carefully selected little parties the Astors invited Eden. In the small drawing room banked with flowers the idea was broached about sending an emissary to talk the matter over with Hitler—some genial, inoffensive person like Lord Halifax (huge land interests) for instance. Eden understood why the *Times* had suddenly raised the issue of the lost German colonies to an extent greater even than Hitler himself, and Eden emphatically expressed his disapproval. Such a step, he insisted, would encourage both Germany and Italy to further aggressions which would ultimately wreck the British Empire.

Nevertheless, the cabinet ministers who had been consulted brought pressure upon Chamberlain and while the Foreign Secretary was in Brussels on a state matter, the Prime Minister announced that Halifax would visit the Führer. Eden was furious and after a stormy session tendered his resignation. At that period, however, Eden's resignation might have thrown England into a turmoil—so Chamberlain mollified him. Public sympathy was with Eden and before he was eased out, the country had to be prepared for it.

In the quiet and subdued atmosphere of the diplomats' drawing rooms in London they tell, with many a chuckle, how Lord Halifax, his bowler firmly on his head, was sent to Berlin and Berchtesgaden in mid-November, 1937, with instructions not to get into any arguments. Lord Halifax, in the mellow judgment of his close friends, is one of the most amiable and charming of the British peers, earnest, well meaning and—not particularly bright.

In Berlin Halifax met Goering, attired for the occasion in a new and bewilderingly gaudy uniform. In the course of their conversation Goering, resting his hands on his enormous paunch, said:

"The world cannot stand still. World conditions cannot be frozen just as they are forever. The world is subject to change."

"Of course not," Lord Halifax agreed amiably. "It's absurd to think that anything can be frozen and no changes made."

"Germany cannot stand still," Goering continued. "Germany must expand. She must have Austria, Czechoslovakia and other countries—she must have oil—"

Now this was a point for argument but the Messenger Extraordinary had been instructed not to get into any arguments; so he nodded and in his best pacifying tone murmured, "Naturally. No one expects Germany to stand still if she must expand."

After Austria was invaded and Halifax was asked by his close friends what he had cooked up over there, he told the above story, expressing the fear that his conversation was probably misunderstood by Goering, the latter taking his amiability to mean that Great Britain approved Germany's plans to swallow Austria. The French Intelligence Service, however, has a different version, most of it collected during February, 1938, which, in the light of subsequent events, seems far more accurate.

Lord Halifax, these secret-service reports state, pledged England to a hands-off policy on Hitler's ambitions in Central Europe if Germany would not raise the question of the return of the colonies for six years. Within that period England estimated that Hitler would have expanded, strengthened his war machine and fought the Soviet Union to a victorious conclusion.

Late in January 1938, Lord and Lady Astor invited some guests for a weekend at Cliveden. The Prime Minister of England came and so did Lord Halifax, Lord Lothian, Tom Jones and J. L. Garvin, editor of the Astor-controlled London *Observer*. When Chamberlain returned to London, he asked Eden to open negotiations with Italy to secure a promise to stop killing British sailors and sinking British merchant vessels in the Mediterranean. During this time the British Foreign Office was issuing statements that Mussolini was "cooperating" in the hunt for the "unidentified" pirates.

British opinion, roused by the sinking of English ships, might hamper deals with the fascist leaders if such attacks were not ended. In return for the cessation of the piratical attacks, Chamberlain was ready to offer recognition of Abyssinia and even loans to Italy to develop her captured territory. It was paying tribute to a pirate chieftain, but Chamberlain was ready to do it to quiet opposition at home to the sinking of British vessels and to give him time in which to develop his policy.

Eden, who had fought for sanctions against the aggressor when Abyssinia was invaded, obeyed orders but insisted that Italy must first get her soldiers out of Spain. He did not want Mussolini to get a stranglehold upon Gibraltar, one of the strategic life lines of the British Empire. Mussolini refused and told the British Ambassador in Rome that he and Great Britain would never to able to get together because Eden insisted on the withdrawal of Italian troops from Spain, and that it might help if a different Foreign Secretary were appointed. Hitler, working closely with Mussolini in the Rome-Berlin axis, also began to press for a different Foreign Secretary but went Mussolini one better. Von Ribbentrop informed Chamberlain that Der Führer was displeased with the English press attacks upon him, Nazis and Nazi aggressions. Der Führer wanted that stopped.

The Foreign Office of the once proud and still biggest empire in the world promptly sent notes to the newspapers in Fleet Street requesting that stories about Nazis and Hitler be toned down "to aid the government," and most of the once proud and independent British newspapers established a "voluntary censorship" at what amounted to an order from Hitler relayed through England's Foreign Office. The explanation the newspapers gave to their staffs was that the world situation was too critical to refuse the government's request and, besides that refusal would probably mean losing routine Foreign Office and other government department news sources. The more than average British citizen doesn't know even today how his government and "independent" press took orders from Hitler.

In the latter part of January, 1938, the French Intelligence Service, still not knowing of the secret deal Halifax had made, learned that Hitler intended to invade Austria late in February and that simultaneously both Italy and Germany, instead of withdrawing troops as they had said they would, planned to intensify their offensive in Spain. When the French Intelligence learned of it, M. Delbos, then French Foreign Minister, and Eden were in Geneva attending a meeting of the Council of the League. Delbos excitedly informed Eden who, never dreaming that Great Britain had not only agreed to sacrifice Austria and betray France but was also double-crossing her own Foreign Minister, telephoned Chamberlain from Geneva.

The Prime Minister listened attentively, thanked him dryly, hung up, and promptly telephoned Sir Eric Phipps, British Ambassador to France. Sir Eric was instructed to get hold of M. Chautemps, the French Premier at the time, and ask that Chautemps instruct Delbos to stop frightening the British Foreign Secretary. But all during February the French Intelligence kept getting more information about the planned invasion of Austria and the proposed intensified offensive in Spain, and relayed it to England with insistent suggestions for joint precautions. Eden in turn relayed it to Chamberlain who always thanked him.

The date set for the invasion was approaching but Eden was still in office and Hitler began to fear that perhaps "perfidious Albion" with all her overtures of friendship might really be double-crossing Germany. If England could send a special emissary to offer to sell out Austria and double-cross her ally France, she might be quite capable of tricking Germany. Simultaneously the Gestapo stumbled upon information that the British Intelligence had reached into the top ranks of the German Army and was working with high officers. Hitler, not knowing how far the British Intelligence had penetrated, shook up his cabinet, made Ribbentrop Secretary for Foreign Affairs, and prepared for war in the event that England was leading him into a trap.

There are records in the British Foreign Office which show that Hitler, before invading Austria, tested England to be sure he wasn't being led into a trap. Von Ribbentrop informed Eden and Chamberlain that Hitler intended to summon Schuschnigg, the Austrian Chancellor, and demand that Austria rearrange her cabinet, take in Dr. Seyss-Inquart and release imprisoned Nazis. Hitler knew that Schuschnigg would immediately rush to England and France for aid. If they turned Austria down it was safe to proceed with the invasion.

The British Foreign Office records show that Schuschnigg did rush to England and France for support, that France was ready to give it, but that England refused, thereby forcing France to keep out of it.

While these frantic maneuvers were going on, the Astor-controlled *Times* and *Observer*, the Nazi and the Italian press simultaneously started a campaign against Eden. The date set for the sacrifice of Austria was approaching and Eden had to go or it might fail. The public, however, was with Eden; so another kind of attack was launched. Stories began to appear about the Foreign Secretary's health. There were sighs, long faces, sad regrets, but Eden stuck to his post in the hope that he could do something. On February 19, Hitler, tired of waiting, bluntly demanded that he be removed, and with the newspaper campaign in full swing, Chamberlain "in response to public opinion" removed him the very next day.

The amiable Lord Halifax was appointed Foreign Secretary. Pro-fascists like A. L. Lennon-Boyd, stanch supporter of Franco and admirer of Hitler and Mussolini, were given ministerial posts.

The Austrian invasion was delayed for three weeks because of the difficulty in getting Eden out. When the news flashed to a startled world that Nazi troops were thundering into a country whose independence Hitler had promised to respect, M. Corbin, the still unsuspecting French Ambassador, rushed to the Foreign Office to arrange for swift joint action. This was at four o'clock in the afternoon of March 11, 1938. Instead of receiving him immediately, Lord Halifax kept him waiting until nine o'clock in the evening. By that time Austria was Nazi territory. There was nothing to do but protest; so Lord Halifax, with a straight face, joined France in a "strong protest." It was not until a week after Austria had been absorbed that the French Intelligence Service learned the details of the Halifax deal and finally understood why England had side-stepped the pleas for joint action and why the French Ambassador had been kept cooling his heels until the occupation of Austria was completed.

From Austria Hitler got more men for his army, large deposits of magnesite, timber forests and enormous water-power resources for electricity. From Czechoslovakia, if he could get it, Hitler would have the Skoda armament works, one of the biggest in the world, factories in the Sudeten area, be next door to Hungarian wheat and Rumanian oil, dominate the Balkans, destroy potential Russian air and troop bases in Central Europe, and place Nazi troops within a few miles of the Soviet border and the Ukrainian wheat fields he has eyed so long.

Five days after Austria was invaded, on March 16, at 3:30 in the afternoon, Lord Halifax personally summoned the Czechoslovakian Minister. At four o'clock the Minister came out of the conference with a dazed and bewildered air. Lord Halifax had made some "suggestions." Revealing complete ignorance of what had happened and was happening in Czechoslovakian politics, Halifax was nevertheless laying down the law.

It was obvious that the British Foreign Secretary was getting orders from someone else, for Halifax suggested that the Central European Republic try to conciliate Germany (which it had been doing for months) and that a German be taken into the cabinet (there were already three in it). On March 22 there was another meeting at which the Minister learned that Halifax wanted the Czech Government to take a Nazi into the cabinet—as Austria took Dr. Seyss-Inquart at Hitler's orders.

This pressure from England for Czechoslovakian Nazis to be given more power in the government was virtually telling the beleaguered little democracy to fashion a strong rope and hang itself. Subsequent events showed that Chamberlain personally supplied the rope.

Then came the historic weekend of March 26–27, 1938.

The walls of the small drawing room at Cliveden House are lined with shelves filled with books. The laughing and chatting guests had gathered there after a delightful dinner. For the Prime Minister of England to go through all sorts of contortions in a game of charades might prove a trifle undignified; so the hostess suggested that they play "musical chairs."

Everyone thought it was a splendid idea and men servants in their impressive blue liveries arranged the chairs in the required order, carefully spacing the distances between them. One of the laughing and bejeweled women took her place at the piano. In "musical chairs" there is one person more than the number of chairs. When the music starts the players march around the chairs. The moment the music stops everyone dives for the nearest chair leaving the extra person standing and subject to the hilarious jibes of the other players and those rooting from the bleachers. It's one of the ways statesmen relax.

The music started and the dour Prime Minister of the greatest empire in the world, the Minister in charge of the Empire's defense measures, the editor of England's most powerful newspaper, the Right Honorable Speaker of the House of Commons, the sister-in-law of England's leading fascist and several others started marching while the piano tinkled its challenging tune. The Prime Minister, perhaps because he is essentially conservative, marched cautiously and stepped quickly between the spaces while Lady Astor eyed him shrewdly and the others suppressed giggles. The Prime Minister tried to maintain at least the dignity of his banking background but managed "to look only a little porky" as one expressed it afterward. Suddenly the music stopped. Everyone lunged for the nearest chair. The Prime Minister managed to get one and plopped into it heavily.

After half an hour or so some of the strategic rulers of Great Britain got a little winded and quit. A conversation started on foreign affairs and most of the wives retired to another room. When the discussion was ended the little Cliveden house party had come to six major decisions which will change the face of the world if successfully carried through.

Those decisions (maneuvers to put some of them into effect have already begun) are:

1. To inform France that England will go to her aid if she is attacked, unless the attack results from a treaty obligation with another power.

2. To introduce peace time conscription in England.

3. To appoint three ministers to coordinate industrial defense (conscription in peace time); supervise military conscription; and, coordinate the "political education of the people" (propaganda).

4. To reach an agreement with Italy to preserve the legitimate interest of both countries in the Mediterranean.

5. To discuss mutual problems with Germany.

6. To express the hope to Germany that her methods of self-assertion be such as will not hinder mutual discussions by arousing British public opinion against her.

The two most important decisions in this plan are the one for the conscription of labor in peace time and the effort to force France to break the Franco-Soviet pact by choosing between England and Russia.

Consider conscription first and the motives behind it:

When any country whose workers are strongly organized starts veering towards fascism, it must either win over the trade-unions in one way or another or destroy them, for rebellious labor can prevent fascism by means of the general strike. British labor is known to hate fascism since it has learned that fascism destroys, among other things, the value of the trade-unions and all that they have gained after many years of struggle. Any veering by England toward fascism and fascist alliances spells trouble with the trade-unions; hence, the decision "to coordinate the political education of the people." This move is particularly necessary since some trade-union leaders, especially in the important armament industry, have already stated publicly that unless the workers were given assurances that the arms labor was manufacturing would be used in defense of democracy and not to destroy it, they would not cooperate.

Hence "the education of the people" and the conscription of labor in peace time which would ultimately lead to government control over the unions. With some variations it is the same procedure followed by Hitler in getting control of the once extremely powerful German trade-unions.

A few days after this historic weekend, the *Times* came out for "national organization" and the wisdom of "national registration." National registration, as the history of fascist countries has shown, is the first step in the conscription of labor. With this opening gun having been fired, it is a safe prophecy that if the Chamberlain government remains in office British labor will witness one of the most determined attacks ever made upon it in its history. All indications point to the ground being laid and it may result in splitting the trade-union movement, for some of the leaders are willing to go with the government while others have already indicated that they will refuse unless they know that it's for democracy and not for fascism.

The second important decision is to exert pressure upon France to break her pact with the Soviet Union—something Hitler has been unsuccessfully trying to accomplish for a long time. At the moment it appears that Great Britain will succeed just as she has already succeeded in breaking the Czechoslovakian-Soviet pact—another rupture Hitler was determined upon.

England has a reputation for shrewd diplomacy. In the past she has used nations and peoples, played one against the other, betrayed, sacrificed, double-crossed in the march of her empire. Since the Cliveden weekend, however, with its resultant intrigues, England has, to all appearances, finally double-crossed herself.

Those who guide her destiny and the destinies of her millions of subjects have apparently come to the conclusion that democracy, as England has known it, cannot survive and that it is a choice between fascism and communism. Under communism, the ruling class to which the Cliveden weekend guests belong, stand to lose their wealth and power. It is the fatuous hope of the economic royalists that under fascism they will still sit on top of the roost, and so the Cliveden weekenders move toward fascism.

Hitler's Fifth Column finds strange allies.

III FRANCE'S SECRET FASCIST ARMY

NEITHER HITLER NOR MUSSOLINI COULD have foreseen the development of a Cliveden set or England's willingness to weaken her own position as the dominant European power by sacrificing Austria and a good portion of Czechoslovakia. The totalitarian powers proceeded on the assumption that when the struggle for control of central Europe, the Balkans and the Mediterranean came they would have to fight.

The Rome-Berlin axis reasoned logically that if, when the expected war broke out, France could be disrupted by a widespread internal rebellion, not only would she be weakened on the battlefield but fascism might even be victorious in the Republic. In preparation for this, the axis sent into France secret agents plentifully supplied with money and arms, and almost succeeded in one of the most amazing plots in history.

*　*　*

The opening scene of events which led directly to the discovery of how far the foreign secret agents had progressed took place in the Restaurant Drouant on the Place Gaillon which is frequented by leaders of Paris' financial, industrial and cultural life.

Precisely at noon, on September 10, 1937, Jacqueline Blondet, an eighteen-year-old stenographer with marcelled hair, sparkling eyes, and heavily rouged lips, passed through the rotating doors of the famous restaurant and turned right as she had been instructed. She had never been in so luxurious a place before—dining rooms done in gray or brown marble with furniture to match. Two steps lead from the gray to the brown room and Mlle. Blondet, not noticing them in her excitement, slipped and would have fallen had not the old wine steward who looks like Charles Dickens, caught and steadied her.

The two men with whom she was lunching were at a table at the far corner of the deserted room. The one who had invited her, François Metenier, a well-known French engineer and industrialist, powerfully built, with sharp eyes, dark hair, and a suave self-assured manner, rose at her approach, smiling at her embarrassment. The other man, considerably younger, was M. Locuty, a stocky, bushy haired man with square jaws and heavy tortoise-shell eyeglasses. He was an engineer at the huge Michelin Tire Works at Clermont-Ferrand where Metenier was an important official. The industrialist introduced the girl merely as "my friend" without mentioning her name.

With the exception of two couples having a late breakfast in the gray marble room, which they could see from their table, the three were alone.

"Shall we have a bottle of Bordeaux?" asked Metenier. "I ordered lunch by 'phone but I thought I would await your presence on the wine."

"Oh, anything you order," said Locuty with an effort at casualness.

"Yes, you order the wine," said the stenographer.

"*Garçon,* a bottle of St. Julien, Château Léoville-Poyferre 1870."

The ghost of Charles Dickens, who had been hovering nearby, bowed and smiled with appreciation of the guest's knowledge of a rare fine wine and personally rushed off to the cellars for the Bordeaux.

When the early lunch was over and the brandy had been set before them, Metenier studied his glass thoughtfully and glanced at the two portly men who had entered the brown dining room and sat some tables away. From the snatches of conversation the three gathered that one was a literary critic and the other a publisher. They were discussing a thrilling detective story just published which the critic insisted was too fantastic.

Metenier said to Locuty:

"You will have to make two bombs. I will take you to a very important man in our organization, a power in France. He will personally give you the material and show you how to make them. Then I will take you to the places where you will leave them. I do not want them to see me."

In low tones, they discussed the bombing of two places. Metenier, a pillar of the church, highly respected in his community and well-known throughout France, cautioned them as they left.

Why the vivacious blond stenographer was permitted to sit in on this conversation, Locuty did not know, unless it was to tempt him, for, as she bade him good-by, she squeezed his hand significantly and said she wanted to see him again.

Metenier drove Locuty to an office building where he introduced him to a man he called "Leon"—actually Alfred Macon, concierge of a building which Metenier and others used as headquarters for their activities. Within a few moments the door of an adjacent room opened and Jean Adolphe Moreau de la Meuse, aristocrat and leading French industrialist, came in. He had a monocle in his right eye which he kept adjusting nervously. His face was deeply marked and lined with heavy bluish pouches under the eyes. With a swift glance he sized up Locuty as Metenier rose.

"This is the gentleman whom I mentioned," he said.

"He understands his mission?" De la Meuse asked.

"Yes," said Locuty. "You will teach me how to make them?"

De la Meuse nodded. "It will be a time bomb which must be set for ten o'clock tomorrow night. There will be nobody in the building at that time, so no one will be hurt."

An hour later Locuty, who had made both bombs and set the timing devices, wrapped them into two neat packages. Metenier took him to the General Confederation of French Employers' Building in the Rue de Presbourg. In accordance with instructions he left one of the packages with the concierge, after which Metenier took him to the Ironmasters' Association headquarters on the Rue Boissiere, where Locuty left the second package.

On the evening of September 11, the General Confederation of French Employers was scheduled to hold a meeting in their building. This meeting was postponed; and, as De la Meuse had assured the Michelin engineer, the concierges and their wives, contrary to custom, were not in their buildings that evening.

At ten o'clock, both bombs exploded. The plans had gone off as arranged except for an accident, the investigation of which made public the whole amazing conspiracy. Two French gendarmes standing near one of the buildings were killed.

Immediately after the bombs exploded, the Employers' Confederation and the Ironmasters' Association issued statements charging the Communists and the Popular Front with being responsible for the outrages and accusing them of planning a reign of terror to seize control of France. The accusations left a profound effect upon the French people despite the Communists' assertions that they never countenance terrorism. The *Sûreté Nationale,* the French Scotland Yard, opened an intensive investigation which was spurred on by the deaths of the unfortunate gendarmes. It was not long before the French people heard of the almost incredibly fantastic plot to destroy the Popular Front and establish fascism in France—a plot directed by leading French industrialists and high army officers cooperating with secret agents of the German and Italian Governments.

The ramifications of the plot are so packed with dynamite in the national and international arena that the French government, under pressure from England as well as from some of its own industrialists, government officials and army officers, has clamped the lid down on further disclosures lest continued publicity seriously affect the delicate balance of international relations.

▩   ▩   ▩

It was obvious from what the police uncovered that it had taken several years to organize the gigantic conspiracy. Within the teeming city of Paris itself, steel and concrete fortresses had been secretly built. Other cities throughout France were similarly ringed in strategic places. Every one of these secret fortresses was stocked with arms and munitions, and throughout the country, once the confessions began, the police found thousands upon thousands of rifles and pistols, millions of cartridges, hundreds of machine guns and sub-machine guns. The fortresses themselves were fitted with secret radio and telephone stations for communication among themselves. Code books and evidence of arms-running from Germany and Italy were found. A vast espionage network and a series of murders were traced to this secret organization whose official name is the "Secret Committee for Revolutionary Action." At their meetings they wore hoods to conceal their identity from one another, like the Black Legion in the United States, and the press promptly named them the "Cagoulards" ("Hooded Ones").

Just how many members the Cagoulards actually have is unknown except to its Supreme Council and probably to the German and Italian Intelligence Divisions. Lists of names totaling eighteen thousand men were turned up by the *Sûreté Nationale,* and the hundreds of steel and concrete fortresses and the arms found in them point to a membership of at least 100,000. The way the fortresses were built and their strategic locations (blowing down the walls of the buildings where the fortresses were hidden would have given them command of streets, squares and government buildings) indicate supervision by high military officials.

When contractors buy enormous quantities of cement for dugouts, when butchers' and bakers' lorries rattle over ancient cobblestones with enormous loads of arms smuggled across German and Italian borders, when thousands of people are drilled and trained in pistol, rifle and machine-gun practice, it is impossible that the competent French Intelligence Service and the *Sûreté Nationale* should not get wind of it.

As far back as September, 1936, the *Sûreté Nationale* knew that some leading French industrialists with the cooperation of the German and Italian Governments were building a military fascist organization within France. Nevertheless it quietly permitted fortresses to be built and stocked with munitions. The General Staff of the French Army, from reports of Intelligence men in Germany and Italy, knew that those countries were smuggling arms into France, but they permitted it to go on. The General Staff knew that some eight hundred concrete fortresses were being built under the supervision of M. Anceaux, a building contractor of Dieppe, and that skilled members of the Secret Committee for Revolutionary Action had been recruited for the building and sworn to secrecy under penalty of death. They knew that these fortresses were equipped with sending and receiving radios, knew that some were within the shadow of military centers, knew that the Cagoulards had a far-flung espionage system. But the French General Staff made no effort to stop it.

The Popular Front Government was in power at the time, and heads of the Supreme War Council apparently preferred a fascist France to a democratic one. In fact, officers and reserve officers of the French Army cooperated with secret agents of their traditional enemy, Germany, to build up this formidable secret army.

The investigating authorities, stunned by their discoveries and the high officials and individuals to whom their investigations led, either did not dare go further with it, or, if they did, suppressed the information. Some of it, however, came out.

At the top of the Cagoulards is a Supreme War Council or General Staff whose members have not been disclosed. Working with them are several other organizations, all with innocent names, as for example the "Society of Studies for French Regeneration." The Cagoulards' activities are divided into broad general lines, each directed by an individual in complete command and embracing:

Buying war materials within France and smuggling war materials into the country from Germany, Italy and Insurgent Spain, along with the simultaneous weaving of an espionage network under Nazi and fascist direction and leadership.

Building concrete fortresses at strategic centers and storing smuggled arms in them.

Military training of secretly organized troops.

Getting the money to carry on these extensive activities.

Extreme care was, and still is, taken to conceal the identities of the ordinary members and especially the leaders. For instance, one of the leaders known to his subordinates as "Fontaine" is in reality Georges Cachier, director of a large company in Paris and chief of the Cagoulards' "Third Bureau," which is in charge of military movements. Cachier is an Officer of the French Legion of Honor and a reserve Lieutenant-Colonel in the French Army.

The Cagoulards are still very active. Members are being recruited with leaders pointing out to the fearful ones that there is nothing to worry about—almost all of those arrested in the early days of the investigation are free, out on bail or kept in a "gentleman's confinement" where they can do virtually as they please. "Our power is great," new members are told.

As is customary in secret terrorist societies, the members are sworn to silence with death as the penalty for indiscretion. The penalty when it is employed is usually administered in American gangster fashion. Each member is allotted to a "cell," the basic unit of the military organization, and assigned to a secretly fortified post for training. One of these posts discovered by the *Sûreté Nationale* was in an old boarding house run by two ancient spinsters with equally ancient guests who spent their time in rockers, knitting and reading and not dreaming that underneath the porch on which they sat so tranquilly was a fortress with enough explosives to blow the whole street to smithereens. Into this particular fortification, the cell members would steal one by one after the old maids had retired, entering by a concealed door three feet thick and electrically operated.

There are two different kinds of cells in the Cagoulards, "heavy" and "light" ones. They differ in the number of men and the quantity of armaments assigned to them. The "light" cell has eight men equipped with army rifles, automatics, hand grenades, and one sub-machine gun; the "heavy" one has twelve men similarly armed but with a machine gun instead of a sub-machine gun. Three cells form a unit, three units a battalion, three battalions a regiment, two regiments a brigade and two brigades a division of two thousand men. The battalions (one hundred and fifty men) are subdivided into squads of fifty to sixty men with ten to twelve cars at their disposal for quick movement throughout the city. These automobile squads are given intensive training.

Members are not required to pay dues, for enough money comes in from industrialists and the German and Italian Governments to eliminate the need of collecting money from members for operating expenses. Every effort is made to function without written communications.

No membership cards are issued. Notices of meetings, drill and rifle practice are issued verbally, and so far as the mass membership is concerned, nothing in writing is placed in their hands.

A twenty-page handbook with instructions on street fighting was issued to group commanders and, lest a copy fall into wrong hands and betray the organization, it was boldly entitled: *Secret Rules of the Communist Party.* The instructions are specific and are based upon the insurrectionary tactics issued to the Nazi Storm Troopers. They fall into six sections: General Remarks; Group Fighting; Section Fighting; Choice of Terrain; Commissariat; and Policing Groups.

One or two excerpts from these instructions for street fighting follow:

> The particular force for street fighting is infantry, provided with automatic weapons and hand grenades. Members of the detachments should be instructed that automatic weapons must always be used in preference. Essential arms are: sub-machine guns, rifles including hunting rifles, hand grenades, revolvers, petards. (Petards are small bombs used for blowing in doors.)

With regard to "mopping up" in houses, the instructions state:

> If the door is barricaded, it must be opened with tools or explosives. If it is a heavy door, break it in by driving a lorry at it. Clean up basements and cellars by throwing bombs down through the air holes or other openings after your men have got into the house. Only after these have exploded should the cellar doors be forced. Then, when ascending the stairs, keep close to the walls while one of your men keeps firing straight up the shaft. Mop up as you go down floor by floor. If necessary, pierce holes in the ceilings and mop up by throwing down hand grenades.

The chief of the Cagoulards' espionage system is Dr. Jean Marie Martin, a bushy-haired stocky man with dark, somber eyes. Dr. Martin usually travels with several false passports and with the utmost secrecy. At the moment he is in Genoa where he went to meet Commendatore Boccalaro, Mussolini's personal representative in charge of smuggling arms into foreign countries.

The preparations by the Rome-Berlin axis point to plans for a fight to a finish between fascist and non-fascist countries. A feeble or disrupted democracy will obviously strengthen the fascist powers in any coming struggle with anti-fascist powers. Germany and Italy, faced on their own borders with a democratic France allied with the Soviet Union in a military defense pact, would face a powerful enemy in the event of war. But if France were torn by a bloody civil war, she would be virtually unable even to defend her borders. Consequently, it is essential for Germany and Italy to weaken and if possible destroy France's democracy.

France and Germany have been traditional enemies in their struggle for land containing raw materials needed by their industries to compete in the world markets. But the growth of the French labor movement and the power of the Popular Front which threatened the control and the profits of French industrialists and financiers, made them find more in common with fascist and Nazi industrialists than with French workers who menaced their economic and political control. The result was that leading French industrialists were willing to cooperate with Nazi and fascist agents to destroy the Popular Front and establish fascism in France. About half of the 200,000,000 francs, which it is estimated the fortresses and arms cost, was contributed by French industrialists. The other half came from the German and Italian Governments.

Germany and Italy sent swarms of secret agents into France to supervise the building of the underground military machine and to carry on intensive espionage with the assistance of the French Army and Government officials who were members of the Hooded Ones. The espionage service was organized by Baron de Potters, an old international spy who travels with two or more passports under the names of Farmer and Meihert. De Potters gets his funds from the Nazis' strongly guarded "Bureau III B," established in Berne, Switzerland at 21 Gewerbestrasse. "Bureau III B" is the official name of this branch of the Gestapo. At the head of it is Boris Toedli whose activities include not only espionage but underground diplomatic intrigue and propaganda. He works directly under Drs. Rosenberg and Goebbels. Toedli supplies not only the Baron but other espionage directors with money and there is plenty of it at his disposal for quick emergency uses. The money is deposited in the *Société des Banques Suisses,* account No. 60941.

The head of the Italian espionage system directing the work in France and cooperating closely with the Nazis is Commendatore Boccalaro, head of the Italian Government's Arsenal in Genoa. One of his specialties is the smuggling of arms into foreign countries.

Boccalaro's history shows that the not so fine Italian hand is interfering in the internal affairs of foreign governments. As far back as 1928, he secretly supplied carloads of arms from the Genoa Arsenal to Hungary, and in 1936 he supplied Yugoslavian terrorists with war materials in efforts to get those countries under Mussolini's sphere of influence. Boccalaro, too, seems to have had reasons to suppress information in at least one case where the death penalty was inflicted upon a member of the Cagoulards.

Among the Hooded Ones who have been found with bullets or knives in them was an arms runner named Adolphe-Augustin Juif, who tried to charge the secret organization a little more than he should for smuggling guns and munitions into France. When the organization threatened him, he advised it not to resort to threats because he knew a little too much.

On February 8, 1937, his bullet-riddled body was found in San Remo, Italy. When Juif's wife, not hearing from him, sought information about his whereabouts, she wrote to Boccalaro, since she knew he was working with the Genoa director. The Italian papers had announced the finding of his body; nevertheless, on March 3, Boccalaro wrote to the murdered man's widow:

"Your husband, my dear friend, is carrying on a special and delicate mission (perhaps in Spain or Germany) and has special reasons of a delicate nature not to inform even his own family where he is at the present moment."

Among the men whom Juif met before he was murdered was Eugène Deloncle, director of the Maritime and River Transport Mortgage Company and one of the most important industrialists in France. Deloncle, a high official in the Cagoulards, used the name of "Grosset" in his conspiratorial activities. The other man whom the murdered Juif met is General Edouard Arthur Duseigneur, former Air Force chief and Military Adviser to the French Air Ministry. The General is one of the military heads of the Cagoulards and frequently met with Baron de Potters.

· · ·

The *Sûreté Nationale,* the French Intelligence Service, and the examining magistrate have documentary evidence that Germany and Italy were and are deliberately conspiring to throw France, as they did Spain, into a civil war. Publication of these documents would have far-reaching effects, internally and externally. Great Britain, however, planning to establish a four-cornered pact between England, France, Germany and Italy, brought pressure to bear upon France to suppress further disclosures about the Cagoulards. To England's pressure was added that of leading French industrialists, financiers, government and army officials. Gradually, news about the Cagoulards is dying out. The real heads of the Hooded Ones either have not been named or, if arrested in the early days of the investigation, have been released on bail. And recruiting for the underground army is still going on.

IV DYNAMITE UNDER MEXICO

MOST PEOPLE IN THE UNITED STATES feel secure from European or Asiatic aggression since wide oceans apparently separate us from the conquering ambitions of a Führer or a Son of the Sun. However, despite our desire to be left in peace, the Rome-Berlin axis, which Japan joined, has cast longing eyes upon the Western Hemisphere. The Monroe Doctrine is of value only so long as aggressor nations feel we are too strong for them to violate it; recent history has shown what pieces of paper are worth.

In the process of trying to get a foothold in the Americas, the Nazis have sent agents into all of the countries, but because most of the Central and South American republics are still resentful of past acts by the "Colossus of the North," they offer the most fertile fields.

The two spots on the Western Hemisphere most vital to the United States are the Panama Canal Zone and Mexico—the Zone because it is our trade and naval life line between the oceans and Mexico because potential enemies could find in it perfect military and naval bases.

Let us see what the totalitarian powers are doing in Mexico:

　　　※　　※　　※

On June 30, 1937, the S.S. "Panuco" of the New York and Cuba Mail Steamship Co. steamed into Tampico, Mexico, from New York with a mysterious cargo consigned to one Armeria Estrada. As soon as she docked, the cargo was quickly transferred to the Atchison, Topeka and Santa Fe Railroad freight car No. 45169, which was awaiting it. A gentleman known around the freight yards as A. M. Cabezut, arranged for the car to leave immediately for the state of San Luis Potosí in the heart of Mexico.

There was no record on the bill of lading to show that the shipper was the Winchester Repeating Arms Company of New Haven, Conn., and that the cargo, ordered on January 23 and February 23, 1937, by an Italian named Benito Estrada, was a large quantity of rifles, pistols and one hundred and forty cases of cartridges for various caliber guns.

When the car arrived in San Luis Potosí, it was met by an elderly, mustached German named Baron Ernst von Merck, who took the shipment to General Saturnino Cedillo, former governor of the state[4] and a well-known advocate of fascism. One week later the elderly German met a carload shipment of "farm implements." When it was unloaded in San Luis Potosi, the farm implements turned out to be dynamite.

Von Merck, who has been Cedillo's right-hand man, was during the World War a German spy stationed in Brussels. A member of Cedillo's staff[5] he traveled constantly between San Luis Potosí, where the arms were cached, and the Nazi Legation in Mexico City.

On December 21, 1937, Baron von Merck flew to Guatemala—the same day that a cargo of arms from Germany was to be landed off the wild jungle coast of Campeche in Southern Mexico.

Guatemala, just south of Mexico, is the most thoroughly organized fascist country in Central or South America. Its chief industries, coffee and bananas, are virtually controlled by Germans, whose enormous

---

4 In May, 1938, Cedillo launched an abortive rebellion and is now being hunted by the Mexican government.

5 After Cedillo's defeat von Merck fled to New York and went to Germany.

plantations overlap into the state of Chiapas, Mexico. But President Jorge Ubico, who is not much of an Aryan, prefers Mussolini's brand of fascism because the Nazi theory of Nordic supremacy does not strike a sympathetic chord in the President's heart. As a result, the Italian Minister to Guatemala is Ubico's adviser on almost all matters of state.

Guiseppe Sotanis, a mysterious Italian officer who sits in the Gran Hotel in San José, Costa Rica, collecting stamps and studying his immaculate fingernails, arranges for shipments of Italian arms into Guatemala. A few months ago Sotanis, the Italian minister to Guatemala, and Ubico met in Guatemala City. Shortly thereafter the Italian arms manufacturing company, Bredda, sent Ubico two hundred eighty portable machine guns, sixty anti-aircraft machine guns and seventy small caliber cannon.

But President Ubico is not hopelessly addicted to one brand of fascism. Nazi ships make no attempt to conceal their landing of arms and munitions at Puerto Barrios. From there they are transported by car, river and horse into the dense chicle forests in the mountain regions, then across the Guatemalan border into Chiapas and Campeche.

* * *

During March, 1938, mysterious activities took place in the heart of the chicle forests in Campeche. The region is a dense jungle inhabited by primitive Indian tribes. There is little reason for anyone to build an airport in this territory, much of which has not even been explored. But if the Mexican Government will instruct its air squadron to go to Campeche and fly forty miles north of the Rio Hondo and a little west of Quintana Roo border, they will find a completed airport in the heart of the chicle jungle; and if they will fly a little due west of the small villages of La Tuxpena and Esperanza in Campeche, they will find two more secret airports.

The Mexican Government knows that arms are being smuggled in through its own ports, across the Guatemalan border, and across the wide, sparsely inhabited two-thousand-mile stretch of American border. Both American and Mexican border patrols have been increased, but it is almost impossible to watch the entire region between Southern California and Brownsville. Few contraband runners are caught, apparently because neither the American nor Mexican Governments seem to know the routes followed or who the leading smugglers are.

On February 12, 1938, José Rebey and his brother Pablo, who live in the Altar district of Sonora and know every foot of the desert, drove to Tucson, Arizona, where they met two unidentified Americans. On February 16, 1938, José Rebey and Francisco Cuen, old and close friends of Gov. Roman Yocupicio, drove a Buick to the sandy, deserted wastes near Sonoyta, just south of the American border where one of the two unidentified Americans delivered a carload of cases securely covered with sheet metal. As soon as the cases were transferred into Rebey's car, he turned back on Sonora's flat, dusty roads, passing Caborca, La Cienega, and turning on the sun-dried rutted road to Ures, which lies parched and dry in the semi-tropical sun.

Ures is the central cache for arms smuggled into Sonora by Yocupicio, and the Rebey brothers and Cuen are among the chief contraband runners. The load they carried that day consisted of Thompson guns and cartridges, and the route followed is the one they generally use. A secondary route used by one of Cuen's chief aids, a police delegate from the El Tiro mine, lies over the roads to Ures by way of Altar.

If in time of war it becomes necessary for guard or patrol work to deflect any troops from the army, or ships from the navy, it is of advantage to the enemy. If a coming war found the United States lined up with the democratic as against the fascist powers and serious uprisings broke out in Mexico, it would require several U. S. regiments to patrol the border and a number of U. S. ships to watch the thousands of miles of coast line to prevent arms running to American countries sympathetic to the Berlin-Rome-Tokyo axis.

* * *

The three fascist powers that have cast longing eyes upon Central and South America have apparently divided their activities in the Americas, with Japan concentrating on the coast lines and the Panama Canal, Germany on the large Central and South American countries and Italy upon the small ones.

In Mexico, Nazi agents work directly with Mexican fascist groups, and have undertaken to carry the brunt of spreading anti-democratic propaganda to turn popular sentiment against the "Colossus of the North," and to develop a receptive attitude toward the totalitarian form of government.

Italy concentrates on espionage, with particular attention to Mexican aid to Loyalist Spain. It was the Italian espionage network in Mexico which learned the course of the ill-fated "Mar Cantabrico" which left New York and Vera Cruz with a cargo of arms for the Loyalists and was intercepted and sunk by an Insurgent cruiser.

Though Germany, even more than Italy, is utilizing her propaganda machine in the Americas' markets, the Japanese are not troubling about that just yet. Their commercial missions seem to be much less interested in establishing business connections than in taking photographs. The chief commercial activity all three countries are intensely interested in is getting concessions from Mexico for iron, manganese and oil—materials essential for war. President Lázaro Cárdenas, however, has stated his dislike of fascism on several occasions. Since Germany, Japan and Italy must obtain these products wherever they can get them, it would be to their advantage if a government more friendly to fascism were in power. But, should that prove impossible, the existence of a strong, fascist movement would have, in time of war, tremendous potentialities for sabotage.

Hence, Mexico is today being battered by pro-fascist propaganda broadcasts from Germany on special short-wave beams, and Nazi and fascist agents surreptitiously meet with discontented generals to weave a network throughout the country.

The radio propaganda is devoted chiefly to selling the wonders of totalitarian government, and to the dissemination of subtle, indirect comments calculated to turn popular feeling against the United States. In addition to regular broadcasts, material printed in Spanish and in German by the *Fichte Bund* with headquarters in Hamburg, Germany, is smuggled into Mexico in commercial shipments. A Nazi bund to direct this propaganda was organized secretly because of the government's unfriendly attitude toward fascism. The bund operates as the *Deutsche Volksgemeinschaft* and its propaganda center functions under the name of the "United German Charities." This organization, on the top floor of the building at 80 Uruguay Street, Mexico City, is actually the "Brown House," in direct contact with Nazi propaganda headquarters in Hamburg.

Some of the propaganda distributed in Mexico is smuggled off Nazi ships docking in Los Angeles, and is transported across the American border by agents working under Hermann Schwinn, director of Nazi activities for the West Coast of the United States. The propaganda sent by Schwinn across the American border is chiefly for distribution around Guaymas, where a special effort is being made to win the sympathy of the people. Meanwhile Yocupicio caches arms in Ures and the bland Japanese continue charting the harbors and coast lines.

The Nazis began to build fascism in Mexico right after Hitler got into power. In 1933 Schwinn called a meeting in Mexicali of several Nazi agents operating out of Los Angeles, including General Rodriguez, and several members of a veterans organization. It was at this meeting that the Mexican Gold shirts were organized. Under the direction of Rodriguez and his right-hand men (Antonio F. Escobar was one of them), the fascist organization drilled and paraded, but little official attention was paid to them. Five years ago few people realized the intensity and possibilities of Nazi propaganda and organization. The only ones in Mexico who watched the growth of the fascist military body were the trade-unionists and the Communists. They remembered what happened in Italy and Germany when the Black Shirts and the Brown Shirts were permitted to grow strong.

On November 20, 1935, Rodriguez and his organization staged a military demonstration in Mexico City, and marched upon the President's palace. Trade-unionists, liberals and Communists barred their way. When the pitched battle was over, five Gold Shirts were dead, some sixty persons wounded, and Rodriguez himself had been stabbed by a woman worker, on her lips the furious cry, "Down with fascism!"

When the Gold Shirt leader was discharged from the hospital, he found that his organization had been made illegal, and he himself exiled. Rodriguez went to El Paso, Texas, and immediately, working through Escobar, set about establishing the "Confederation of the Middle Class" to take over now the illegal Gold Shirt work and consolidate the various Mexican fascist groups. Its headquarters was established at 40 Passo de la Reforma.

Rodriguez kept in touch with Schwinn through Henry Allen, a native American of San Diego, who acts as liaison man. It was Allen, on orders from Schwinn, who last year secretly met in Guaymas Ramon F. Iturbe, a member of the Mexican Chamber of Deputies. Iturbe is in constant touch with the fascist groups in Mexico City.

The Gold Shirts smuggled arms into Mexico along the border between Laredo and Brownsville, and cached them in Monterrey. On January 31,

1938, Gold Shirts attempted to attack Matamoros, near Brownsville. A Mexican policeman was killed and another wounded in the fighting. Two days later Gold Shirts surrounded Reynosa, some distance west of Matamoros, but met peasants armed with rifles, pistols and knives. The fascists withdrew and Rodriguez vanished, only to appear in San Diego, California, on February 19, 1938 for a secret meeting with Plutarco Elias Calles, the former President of Mexico. After a three-hour conference Rodriguez went to Los Angeles, met Schwinn, and proceeded to Mission, Texas, where he established new headquarters.

A few days after these conferences, he sent two men into Mexico under forged passports to discuss closer cooperation among the fascist leaders. The men sent into Mexico were an American named Mario Baldwin, one of Rodriguez's chief assistants, and a Mexican named Sanchez Yanez. They established headquarters at 31 José Joaquin Herrera, apartment 1-T, and met for their secret conferences in Jesus de Avila's tailor shop at 22 Isabel la Catolico.

In the latter part of June, 1935, an amiable bar fly arrived in Mexico City from Berlin as civilian attaché to the German Legation. A civilian attaché is the lowest grade in the diplomatic ranks and the salary is just about enough to keep him going. Nevertheless, Dr. Heinrich Northe, at that time not quite thirty, and not especially well-to-do, established a somewhat luxurious place at 64 Tokyo St. and bought a private airplane for "pleasure jaunts" about Mexico. Northe is seldom at the Nazi Legation. He is more apt to be found in Sonora, where Yocupicio is storing arms and where the Japanese fishing fleet is active, or in Acapulco, whose harbor fascinates the Japanese. He used to make frequent visits to Cedillo just before the General started his rebellion. On March

4, 1938, Northe took off "for a vacation" in the Panama Canal Zone. He stopped off in Guatemala on the way down.

The persistently vacationing commercial attaché, before coming to Mexico, was part of the Gestapo network in Moscow and Bulgaria. Immediately after the Nazis got control of Germany, Northe went into the German "diplomatic service," and was one of the first secret agents sent to the German Embassy in Moscow. The Russian secret service apparently watched him a little too closely, for he was shifted to Sofia, Bulgaria, where he bought a private plane and flew wherever he wished. In 1935, when the signers of the "anti-Communist pact" decided to concentrate upon Mexico, Northe was transferred to Mexico City.

One of Northe's chief aids is a German adventurer who was a spy during the World War. When the War ended, Hans Heinrich von Holleuffer, of 36 Danubio St., Mexico City, worked hard at earning a dishonest penny in Republican Germany. When the law got after him, he skipped to Mexico, where, without even pausing for breath, he went to work on his fellow countrymen in the New World. Berlin asked for his arrest and extradition and von Holleuffer fled to Guatemala. That was in 1926. He came back to Mexico in 1931 under the name of Hans Helbing.

When Hitler got into power von Holleuffer's brother-in-law became a high official in the Gestapo. Since there was no danger of the Nazis extraditing him on charges of fraud and forgery, Hans Helbing became Hans Heinrich von Holleuffer again and, without any visible means of support, established a swanky residence at the above address, got an expensive automobile, a chauffeur, and some very good-looking maids. Since he has not defrauded anyone lately, the German colony in Mexico still wonders how he does it.

He does it by being in charge of arms smuggling from Germany to Mexican fascists. During the latter part of December, 1937, he directed the unloading of one of the heaviest cargoes of arms yet shipped into Mexico. Northe had informed von Holleuffer that a German vessel whose name even Northe had not yet been given, would be ready to land a cargo of guns, munitions and mountain artillery somewhere along the wild and deserted coast of Campeche where there are miles of shore with not even an Indian around. Von Holleuffer was instructed to arrange for unloading the cargo and having it removed into the interior.

On December 19, 1937, von Holleuffer arranged a meeting in Mexico City with Julio Rosenberg of 13 San Juan de Letran and Curt Kaiser at 34 Bolivar, the latter's home. He offered them fifty thousand pesos to take the contraband off the boat and transport it through the chicle jungles to the destination he would give them.

⬛　⬛　⬛

Shortly after the Japanese-Nazi pact was signed, the Japanese Government arranged with the somewhat naive Mexican Government for Japanese fishing experts to conduct "scientific explorations" along Mexico's Pacific Coast in return for teaching Mexicans how to catch fish scientifically. The agreement provided that two Japanese, J. Yamashito and Y. Matsui, be employed by the Mexican Government for the exploratory work.

Matsui arrived in Mexico in 1936 and immediately became interested in the fish situation at Acapulco, which from a naval standpoint has the best harbor on the entire long stretch of Mexico's Pacific coast line. In February, 1938, he decided that it was important to the west-coast shrimp-fishing studies for him to do some exploratory work along the northeast part of the Mexican coast, near the American border, and there he went.

Immediately after the agreement was signed, three magnificent fishing boats, the "Minatu Maru," the "Minowa Maru" and the "Saro Maru," which had been hovering out on the Pacific while the negotiations were going on, appeared in Guaymas. Their captains reported to the Nippon

Suisan Kaisha, a fishing company with headquarters in Guaymas. Eighty per cent of this company's stock is owned by the Japanese Government.

Each ship is equipped with large fish bins which can easily be turned into munition carriers, each has powerful short-wave sending and receiving sets; and each has extraordinarily long cruising powers ranging from three to six thousand miles. These boats do not do much fishing. They confine themselves to "exploring," which includes the taking of soundings of harbors, especially Magdalena Bay. Apparently the explorers want to know how deep the fish can swim and whether there are any rocks or ledges in their way.

That Germany, Japan and Italy are not working toward peaceful ends in Mexico is slowly dawning upon the Mexican Government. Influential government and trade-union leaders have repeatedly shown their dislike of Nazism and fascism and have urged propaganda against them.

On the morning of October 5, 1937, Freiherr Riedt von Collenberg, Nazi minister to Mexico, telephoned the Japanese and Italian ministers to suggest a joint meeting to discuss steps to counteract the attacks on fascism and their countries. The Japanese minister, Sacchiro Koshda, suave and skilled in such matters, thought it would not be wise to meet in any of the legations. The Italian minister suggested the offices of the Italian Union on San Cosne Avenue.

At half past one in the afternoon of October 7, the ministers arrived, each in a taxi instead of the legation car which carries a conspicuous diplomatic license plate. At this secret meeting which lasted until after four, they concluded that it would be unwise for them personally to take any steps to counteract the anti-fascist activities—that it would be wiser to work indirectly through fascist organizations like the Confederation of the Middle Class and its associated bodies. A few days earlier each minister had received a letter from several organizations allied with the Confederation of the Middle Class. It was an offer to help the Berlin-Tokyo-Rome combination. A free translation of the passage which the ministers discussed (from the letter received by the Japanese minister which I now have) follows:

"We, exactly like the representatives of the three powers, love our Fatherland and are disposed to any sacrifice to prevent the intervention of these elements [Jews and Communists] in our politics, in which, unfortunately, they have begun to have great influence. And we will employ, and are employing, all legal methods of struggle to make an end of them."

The phrase "legal methods" is frequently employed by those who suggest illegal activity. The German Minister knew that the *Union Nacionalista Mexicana,* one of the signers of the letter, was run by Escobar, and that Carmen Calero, 12 Place de la Concepcion, Mexico City, an elderly woman physician active in many fascist organizations, was a member of the *Partido Anti-reelectionista Accion,* another of the signers.

One month later the various fascist groups got enough money to launch an intensive pro-fascist drive under the usual guise of fighting Communism. José Luis Noriega, Secretary of the Nationalist Youth of Mexico, which also signed the letters to the ministers, left for the United States to organize an anti-Cárdenas drive. At the same time, Carmen Calero left on a mysterious mission to Puebla on November 12, 1937, with a letter from Escobar to J. Trinidad Mata, publisher of the local paper *Avance.* She carried still another letter addressed to their "distinguished comrades," without mentioning names, and signed by both Escobar and Ovidio Pedrero Valenzuela, President of the *Accion Civica Nacionalista.* The "distinguished comrades" to whom she presented the letter were the Nazi honorary consul in Puebla, Carl Petersen, Avenida 2, Oriente 15, and a Japanese agent named L. Yuzinratsa with whom the consul has been in repeated conferences.

Six weeks after the secret meeting of the Japanese, German and Italian ministers, and one week after she went to Puebla, Dr. Carmen Calero got twenty-two kilos of dynamite and stored it in a house at 39 Juan de la Mateos, in Mexico City. She, her sister, Colonel Valenzuela, and four others, met at her home and laid plans to assassinate President Cárdenas by blowing up his train when he left on a proposed trip to Sonora.

On November 18, 1937, the secret police made a series of simultaneous raids upon Dr. Calero's and Valenzuela's homes and the house where the dynamite was cached. They arrested everyone in the houses. But once the arrests had been made, the Mexican Government found itself in a quandary. To bring the prisoners to trial would involve foreign governments and create an international scandal; so Cárdenas personally ordered the secret police to release them.

The arrests, however, scared the wits out of the ministers, and their horror was not lessened when they discovered that the letters from the fascist organizations had vanished from their files. They wouldn't even answer the telephone when one of the released fascist leaders called. It was then that the Mexican fascists decided to send a special messenger to Francisco Franco in Spain (November 30, 1937) with the request that Franco intercede to get money from Hitler to help overthrow Cárdenas, since the Nazi minister was too scared to cooperate. The special messenger was Fernando Ostos Mora. He never got there.

V SURROUNDING THE PANAMA CANAL

THERE IS A LITTLE SHIRT SHOP in Colon, Panama, on Calle 10a between Avenida Herrera and Avenida Amador Guerrero, whose red and black painted shingle announces that Lola Osawa is the proprietor.

Across the street from her shirt shop, where the red light district begins, is a bar frequented by natives, soldiers and sailors. Tourists seldom go there, for it is a bit off the beaten track. In front of the bar is a West Indian boy with a tripod and camera with a telescopic lens. He never photographs natives, and wandering tourists pass him by, but he is there every day from eight in the morning until dark. His job is to photograph everyone who shows an undue interest in the little shirt shop and particularly anyone who enters or leaves it. Usually he snaps your picture from across the street, but if he misses you he darts across and waits to take another shot when you come out.

I saw him take my picture when I entered the store. It was almost high noon and Lola was not yet up. The business upon which she and her husband are supposed to depend for a living was in the hands of two giggling young Panamanian girls who sat idly at two ancient Singer sewing machines.

"You got shirts?" I asked.

Without troubling to rise and wait on me, they pointed to a glass case stretched across the room and barring quick entrance to the shop proper. I examined the assortment in the case, counting a total of twenty-eight shirts.

"I don't especially like these," I said. "Got any others?"

"No more," one of them giggled.

"Where's Lola?"

"Upstairs," the other said, motioning with her thumb to the ceiling.

"Looks like you're doing a rushing business, eh?" They looked puzzled and I explained: "Busy, eh?"

"Busy? No. No busy."

There is little work for them and neither Lola nor they care a whoop whether or not you buy any of the shop's stock of twenty-eight shirts. Lola herself pays little attention to the business from which she obviously cannot earn enough to pay the rent, let alone keep herself and her husband, pay two girls and a lookout.

The little shirt shop is a cubbyhole about nine feet square, its wooden walls painted a pale, washed-out blue. A deck which cuts the store's height in half, forms a little balcony which is covered by a green and yellow print curtain stretched across it. To the right, casually covered by another print curtain, is a red painted ladder by which the deck is reached. On the deck, at the extreme left, where it is not perceptible from the street or the shop, is another tiny ladder which reaches to the ceiling.

If you stand on the ladder and press against the ceiling directly over it, a well-oiled trap door will open soundlessly and lead you into Lola's bedroom above the shop. In front of the window with the blue curtain is a worn bed, the hard mattress neatly covered with a counterpane. At the head of the mattress is a mended tear. It is in this mattress that Lola hides photographs of extraordinary military and naval importance. I saw four of them.

The charming little seamstress is one of the most capable of the Japanese espionage agents operating in the Canal Zone area. Lola Osawa is not her right name. She is Chiyo Morasawa, who arrived at Balboa from Yokahama on the Japanese steamship "Anyo Maru" on May 24, 1929, and promptly disappeared for almost a year. When she appeared again, she was Lola Osawa, seamstress. She has been an active Japanese agent for almost ten years, specializing in getting photographs of military importance. Her husband, who entered Panama without a Panamanian visa on his passport, is a reserve officer in the Japanese Navy. He lives with Lola in the room above the shop, never does any work though he passes as a merchant, and is always wandering around with a camera. Occasionally he vanishes to Japan. His last trip was in 1935. At that time he stayed there over a year.

※　※　※

To defend the ten-mile-wide and forty-six-mile-long strip of land, lakes and canal which the Republic of Panama leased to the United States "in perpetuity," the army, navy and air corps have woven a network of secret fortifications, laid mines and placed anti-aircraft guns. Foreign spies and international adventurers play a sleepless game to learn these military and naval secrets. The Isthmus is a center of intrigue, plotting, conniving, conspiracy and espionage, with the intelligence departments of foreign governments bidding high for information. For the capture or disablement of the Canal by an enemy would mean that American ships would have to go around the Horn to get from one coast to another—a delay which in time of war might prove to be the difference between victory and defeat.

Because of the efficiency and speed of modern communication and transportation, any region within five hundred to a thousand miles of a military objective is considered in the "sensitive zone," especially if it is of great strategic importance. Hence, espionage activities embrace Central and South American Republics which may have to be used by an enemy as a base of operations. Costa Rica, north of the Canal, and Colombia, south of it, are beehives of secret Japanese, Nazi and Italian activities. Special efforts are made to buy or lease land "for colonization," but the land chosen is such that it can be turned into an air base almost overnight.

For decades Japanese in the Canal Zone area have been photographing everything in sight, not only around the Canal, but for hundreds of miles north and south of it; and the Japanese fishing fleet has taken soundings of the waters and harbors along the coast. Since the conclusion of the Japanese-Nazi "anti-Communist pact," Nazi agents have been sent to German colonies in Central and South America to organize them, carry on propaganda and cooperate secretly with Japanese agents. Italy, which had been only mildly interested in Central America, has become extremely active in cultivating the friendship of Central American Republics since she joined the Tokyo-Berlin tie-up. Let me illustrate:

The recognized vulnerability of the Canal has caused the United States to plan another through Nicaragua. The friendship of the Nicaraguan Government and people, therefore, is of great importance to us from both a commercial and a military standpoint. It is likewise of importance to others.

Italy undertook to gain Nicaragua's friendship when she joined the Japanese-Nazi line-up. First, she offered scholarships, with all expenses paid, for Nicaraguan students to study fascism in Italy. Then, on December 14, 1937, about one month after a secret Nazi agent arrived in Central America with orders to step on the propaganda and organizational activity, the Italian S.S. "Leme" sailed out of Naples with a cargo of guns, armored cars, mountain artillery, machine guns and a considerable amount of munitions.

On January 11, 1938, the Secretary of the Italian Legation in San José, Costa Rica, flew to Managua, Nicaragua, to witness the delivery of arms which arrived in Managua on January 12, 1938. Diplomatic representatives do not usually witness purely business transactions, but this was a shipment worth $300,000 which the Italian Government knew Nicaragua could not pay. But, as one of the results, Italy today has a firm foothold in the country through which the United States hopes to build another Canal. The international espionage underground world, which knew that the shipment of arms was coming, has it that Japan, Germany and Italy split the cost of the arms among themselves to gain the friendship of the Nicaraguan Government.

A flood of Nazi propaganda sent on short-wave beams is directed at Central and South America from Germany. In Spanish, German, Portuguese and English, regular programs are sent across at government expense. Government subsidized news agencies flood the newspapers with "news dispatches" which they sell at a nominal price or give away. The programs and the "news dispatches" explain and glorify the totalitarian form of government, and since many of the sister "republics" are dictatorships, they are ideologically sympathetic and receptive.

The Nazis are strong in Colombia, south of the Canal, with a Bund training regularly in military maneuvers at Cali. Since the Japanese-Nazi pact, the Japanese have established a colony of several hundred at Corinto in the Cauca Valley, thirty miles from Cali.

The Japanese colony was settled on land carefully chosen—long, level, flat acres which overnight can be turned into an air base for a fleet landed from an airplane carrier or assembled on the spot. And it is near Cali that Alejandro Tujun, a Japanese in constant touch with the Japanese Foreign Office, is at this writing dickering for the purchase of 400,000 acres of level land for "colonization." On such an acreage enough military men could be colonized to give the United States a first-class headache in time of war. It is two hours flying time from Cali to the Canal.

The entrances on either side of the Panama Canal are secretly mined. The location of these mines is one of the most carefully guarded secrets of the American navy and one of the most sought after by international spies.

The Japanese, who have been fishing along the West Coast and Panamanian waters for years, are the only fishermen who find it necessary to use sounding lines to catch fish. Sounding lines are used to measure the depths of the waters and to locate submerged ledges and covered rocks in this once mountainous area. Any fleet which plans to approach the Canal or use harbors even within several hundred miles north or south of the Canal must have this information to know just where to go and how near to shore they can approach before sending out landing parties.

The use of sounding lines by Japanese fishermen and the mysterious going and comings of their boats became so pronounced that the Panamanian Government could not ignore them. It issued a decree prohibiting all aliens from fishing in Panamanian waters.

In April, 1937, the "Taiyo Maru," flying the American flag but manned by Japanese, hauled up her anchor in the dead of night and with all lights out chugged from the unrestricted waters into the area where the mines are generally believed to be laid. The "Taiyo" operated out of San Diego, California, and once established a world's record of being one hundred and eleven days at sea without catching a single fish. The captain, piloting the boat from previous general knowledge of the waters rather than by chart, unfortunately ran aground. The fishing vessel was stranded on a submerged ledge and couldn't get off.

In the morning the authorities found her, took off her captain and crew—all of whom had cameras—and asked why the boat was in restricted waters.

"I didn't know where I was," said the captain. "We were fishing for bait."

"But bait is caught in the daytime by all other fishermen," the officials pointed out.

"We thought we might catch some at night," the captain explained.

░ ░ ░

Since 1934, when rumors of the Japanese-Nazi pact began to circulate throughout the world, the Japanese have made several attempts to get a foothold right at the entrance to the Canal on the Pacific side. They have moved heaven and earth for permission to establish a refrigeration plant on Taboga Island, some twelve miles out on the Pacific Ocean and facing the Canal. Taboga Island would make a perfect base from which to study the waters and fortifications along the coast and the islands between the Canal and Taboga.

When this and other efforts failed and there was talk of banning alien fishing in Panamanian waters, Yoshitaro Amano, who runs a store in Panama and has far flung interests all along the Pacific coasts of Central and South America, organized the Amano Fisheries, Ltd. In July, 1937, he built in Japan the "Amano Maru," as luxurious a fishing boat as ever sailed the seas. With a purring diesel engine, it has the longest cruising range of any fishing vessel afloat, a powerful sending and receiving radio with a permanent operator on board, and an extremely secret Japanese invention enabling it to detect and locate mines.

Like all other Japanese in the Canal Zone area, Amano, rated a millionaire in Chile, goes in for a little photography. In September, 1937, word spread along the international espionage grapevine that Nicaragua, through which the United States was planning another Canal, had some sort of peculiar fortifications in the military zone at Managua.

Shortly thereafter the Japanese millionaire appeared at Managua with his expensive camera and headed straight for the military zone. Thirty minutes after he arrived (8:OO a.m. of October 7, 1937), he was in a Nicaraguan jail charged with suspected espionage and with taking pictures in prohibited areas.

I mention this incident because the luxurious boat was registered under the Panamanian flag and immediately began a series of actions so peculiar that the Republic of Panama canceled the Panamanian registry. The "Amano" promptly left for Puntarenas, Costa Rica, north of the Canal, which has a harbor big enough to take care of almost all the fleets in the world. Many of the Japanese ships went there, sounding lines and all, when alien fishing was prohibited in Panamanian waters. Today the "Amano Maru" is a mystery ship haunting Puntarenas and the waters between Costa Rica and Panama and occasionally vanishing out to sea with her wireless crackling constantly.

⁂

Some seventy fishing vessels operating out of San Diego, California, fly the American flag. San Diego is of great importance to a potential enemy because it is a naval as well as an air base. Of these seventy vessels flying the American flag, ten are either partially or entirely manned by Japanese.

Let me illustrate how boats fly the American flag:

On March 9, 1937, the S.S. "Columbus" was registered as an American fishing vessel under certificate of registry No. 235,912, issued at Los Angeles. The vessel is owned by the Columbus Fishing Company of Los Angeles. The captain, R. I. Suenaga, is a twenty-six-year-old Japanese, born in Hawaii and a full-fledged American citizen. The navigator and one sailor are also Japanese, born in Hawaii but American citizens. The crew of ten consists entirely of Japanese born in Japan.

The ten boats which fly the American flag but are manned by Japanese crews are: "Alert," "Asama," "Columbus," "Flying Cloud," "Magellan," "Oipango," "San Lucas," "Santa Margarita," "Taiyo," "Wesgate."

Each boat carries a short-wave radio and has a cruising range of from three to five thousand miles, which is extraordinary for just little fishing boats. They operate on the high seas and where they go, only the master and crew and those who send them know. The only time anyone gets a record of them is when they come in to refuel or repair.

In the event of war half a dozen of these fishing vessels, stretched across the Pacific at intervals of five hundred or a thousand miles, would make an excellent system of communication for messages which could be relayed from one to another and in a few moments reach their destination.

In Colón on the Atlantic side and in Panama on the Pacific, East and West literally meet at the crossroads of the world. The winding streets are crowded with the brown and black people who comprise three-fourths of Panama's population. On these teeming, hot, tropical streets are some three hundred Japanese storekeepers, fishermen, commission merchants and barbers—few of whom do much business, but all of whom sit patiently in their doorways, reading the newspapers or staring at the passer-by.

I counted forty-seven Japanese barbers in Panama and eight in Colón. In Panama they cluster on Avenida Central and Calle Carlos A. Mendoza. On both these streets rents are high and, with the exception of Saturdays when the natives come for haircuts, the amount of business the barbers do does not warrant the three to five men in each shop. Yet, though they earn scarcely enough to meet their rent, there is not a lowly barber among them who does not have a Leica or Contax camera with which, until the sinking of the "Panay," they wandered around, photographing the Canal, the islands around the Canal, the coast line, and the topography of the region.

They live in Panama with a sort of permanence, but nine out of ten do not have families—even those advanced in years. Periodically some of them take trips to Japan, though, if you watch their business carefully, you know they could not possibly have earned enough to pay for their passage. And those in the outlying districts don't even pretend to have a business. They just sit and wait, without any visible means of support. It is not until you study their locations, as in the Province of Chorrera, that you find they are in spots of strategic military or naval importance.

Since there were so many barbers in Panama, the need for an occasional gathering without attracting too much attention became apparent. And so the little barber, A. Sonada, who shaves and cuts hair at 45 Carlos A. Mendoza Street, organized a "labor union," the Barbers' Association. The Association will not accept barbers of other nationalities but will allow Japanese fishermen to attend meetings. They meet on the second floor of the building at 58 Carlos A. Mendoza Street, where many of the fishermen live. At their meetings one guard stands outside the room and another downstairs at the entrance to the building.

On hot Sunday afternoons when the Barbers' Association gathers, the diplomatic representatives of other nations are usually taking a siesta or are down at the beach, but Tetsuo Umimoto, the Japanese Consul, climbs the stairs in the stuffy atmosphere and sits in on the deliberations of the barbers and visiting fishermen. It is the only barbers' union I ever heard of whose deliberations were considered important enough for a diplomatic representative to attend. This labor union has another extraordinary custom. It has a special fund to put competitors up in business. Whenever a Japanese arrives in Panama, the Barbers' Association opens a shop for him, buys the chairs—provides him with everything necessary to compete with them for the scarce trade in the shaving and shearing industry!

At these meetings the barber Sonada, who is only a hired hand, sits beside the Japanese Consul at the head of the room. Umimoto remains standing until Sonada is seated. When another barber, T. Takano, who runs a little hole-in-the-wall shop and lives at 10 Avenida B, shows up, both Sonada and the Consul rise, bow very low and remain standing until he motions them to be seated. Maybe it's just an old Japanese custom, but the Consul does not extend the same courtesy to the other barbers.

In attendance at these guarded meetings of the barbers' union and visiting fishermen, is Katarino Kubayama, a gentle-faced, soft-spoken, middle-aged businessman with no visible business. He is fifty-five years old now and lives at Calle Colón, Casa No. 11.

※ ※ ※

Way back in 1917 Kubayama was a barefoot Japanese fisherman like the others now on the west coast. One morning two Japanese battleships appeared and anchored in the harbor. From the reed- and vegetation covered jungle shore, a sun-dried, brown *panga* was rowed out by the barefooted fisherman using the short quick strokes of the native. His brown, soiled dungarees were rolled up to his calves; his shirt, open at the throat, was torn and his head was covered by a ragged straw hat.

The silvery notes of a bugle sounded. The crew of the flagship lined up at attention. The officers, including the Commander, also waited stiffly at attention while the fisherman tied his *panga* to the ship's ladder. As Kubayama clambered on board, the officers saluted. With a great show of formality they escorted him to the Commander's quarters, the junior officer following behind at a respectful distance. Two hours later Kubayama was escorted to the ladder again, the trumpet sounded its salute, and the ragged fisherman rowed away—all conducted with a courtesy extended only to a high ranking officer of the Japanese navy.

Today Kubayama works closely with the Japanese Consul. Together they call upon the captains of Japanese ships whenever they come to Panama, and are closeted with them for hours at a time. Kubayama says he is trying to sell supplies to the captains.

Japanese in the Canal Zone area change their names periodically or come with several passports all prepared. There is, for instance, Shoichi Yokoi, who commutes between Japan and Panama without any commercial reasons. On June 7, 1934, the Japanese Foreign Office in Tokyo issued passport No. 255,875 to him under the name of Masakazu Yokoy with permission to visit all Central and South American countries. Though he had permission for all, he applied only for a Panamanian visa (September 28, 1934), after which he settled down for a while among the fishermen and barbers. On July 11, 1936, the Foreign Office in Tokyo handed Yokoy another passport under the name of Shoichi Yokoi, together with visas which filled the whole passport and overflowed onto several extra pages. Shoichi or Masakazu is now traveling with both passports and a suitcase full of film for his camera.

Several years ago a Japanese named T. Tahara came to Panama as the traveling representative of a newly organized company, the Official Japanese Association of Importers and Exporters for Latin America, and established headquarters in the offices of the Boyd Bros, shipping agency in Panama.

Nelson Rounsevell, publisher of the *Panama American*, who has fought Japanese colonization in Canal areas, printed a story that this big businessman got very little mail, made no efforts to establish business contacts and, in talking with the few businessmen he met socially, showed a complete lack of knowledge about business. Tahara was talked about and orders promptly came through for him to return to Japan.

This was in 1936. Half a year later, a suave Japanese named Takahiro Wakabayashi appeared in Panama as the representative of the Federation of Japanese Importers and Exporters, the same organization under a slightly changed name. Wakabayashi checked into the cool and spacious Hotel Tivoli, run by the United States Government on Canal Zone territory and, protected by the guardian wings of the somewhat sleepy American Eagle, washed up and made a beeline for the Boyd Bros. office, where he was closeted with the general manager for over an hour.

Wakabayashi's business interests ranged from taking pictures of the Canal in specially chartered planes, to negotiating for manganese deposits and attempting to establish an "experimental station to grow cotton in Costa Rica."

The big manganese-and-cotton-photographer man fluttered all over Central and South America, always with his camera. One week he was in San José, Costa Rica; the next he made a hurried special flight to Bogotá, Colombia (November 12, 1937); then back to Panama and Costa Rica. He finally got permission from Costa Rica to establish his experimental station.

In obtaining that concession he was aided by Giuseppe Sotanis, an Italian gentleman wearing the fascist insignia in the lapel of his coat, whom he met at the Gran Hotel in San José. Sotanis, a former Italian artillery officer, is a nattily dressed, slender man in his early forties who apparently does nothing in San José except study his immaculate finger nails, drink Scotch-and-sodas, collect stamps and vanish every few months only to reappear again, still studying his immaculate finger nails. It was Sotanis who arranged for Nicaragua to get the shipment of arms and munitions which I mentioned earlier.

This uncommunicative Italian stamp collector paved the way for Wakabayashi to meet Raul Gurdian, the Costa Rican Minister of Finance, and Ramon Madrigal, Vice-president of the government-owned National Bank and a prominent Costa Rican merchant. Shortly after Costa Rica gave Wakabayashi permission to experiment with his cotton growing, both the Minister of Finance and the Vice-president of the government bank took trips to Japan.

The ink was scarcely dry on the agreement to permit the Japanese to experiment in cotton growing before a Japanese steamer appeared in Puntarenas with twenty-one young and alert Japanese and a bag of cotton seed. They were "laborers," Wakabayashi explained. The "laborers" were put up in first-class hotels and took life easy while Wakabayashi and one of the laborers started hunting a suitable spot on which to plant their bag of seed. All sorts of land was offered to them, but Wakabayashi wanted no land anywhere near a hill or a mountain. He finally found what he wanted half-way between Puntarenas and San José—long, level, flat acres. He wanted this land at any price, finally paying for it an annual rental equal to the value of the acres.

The twenty-one "laborers" who had been brought from Chimbota, Peru, where there is a colony of twenty thousand Japanese, planted an acre with cotton seed and sat them down to rest, imperturbable, silent, waiting. The plowed land is now as smooth and level as the acres at Corinto in Colombia, south of the Canal.

The harbor at Puntarenas, as I mentioned earlier, would make a splendid base of operations for an enemy fleet. Not far from shore are the flat, level acres of the "experimental station" and the twenty-one Japanese who could quickly turn these smooth acres into an air base. It is north of the Panama Canal and within two hours flying time of it, as Corinto is south of the Canal and within two hours flying time.

The Boyd Bros, steamship agency, to which Tahara and Wakabayashi went immediately upon arrival, is an American concern. The manager, with whom each was closeted, is Hans Hermann Heildelk of Avenida Peru, No. 64, Panama City, and, though efforts have been made to keep it secret, part owner of the agency. Heildelk is also the son-in-law of Ernst F. Neumann, the Nazi Consul to Panama.

On November 15, 1937, Heildelk returned from Japan by way of Germany. Five days later, on November 20, 1937, his father-in-law, who, besides being Nazi Consul, owns in partnership with Fritz Kohpcke, one of the largest hardware stores in Panama, told his clerks that he and his partner would work a little late that night. Neither partner went out to eat and the corrugated sliding door of the store, at Norte No. 54 in the heart of the Panamanian commercial district, was left open about three feet from the ground so that passers-by could not see inside unless they stooped deliberately.

At eight o'clock a car drew up at the corner of the darkened street in front of Neumann & Kohpcke, Ltd. Two unidentified men, Heildelk and Walter Scharpp, former Nazi Consul at Colón who had also just returned from Germany, stepped out, and stooping under the partly open door, entered the store. Once inside Scharpp quietly assumed command. To all practical purposes they were on German territory, for the Nazi consulate office was in the store.

Scharpp announced that the group had been very carefully chosen because of their known loyalty to Nazi Germany and because of their desire to promote friendship for Germany in Latin American countries and to cooperate with the Japanese, who had their own organization functioning efficiently in Central and South America.

"Some of these countries are already friendly," said Scharpp, "and we can work undisturbed provided we do not interfere in the Panama Canal Zone. It is North American territory, and you will have trouble from their officials and intelligence officers as well as political pressure from the States. You understand?"

"Panama is friendly to North America," said Kohpcke.

"Precisely. At the present time it is not wise to do much more than broadcast, but at a propitious time we shall be able to explain National Socialism to the Panamanians."

He looked at Kohpcke, whose left eyelid droops more than his right, giving him the appearance of being perpetually sleepy. Kohpcke looked at Neumann.

"Tonight we want to organize a Bund in Panama. In a few days I am going to Costa Rica to organize another and then leave for Valparaiso."

The others nodded. They had been informed that Scharpp was to have complete charge of Nazi activities from Valparaiso to Panama. That night they established *Der Deutsch-Ausländische Nazi Genossenschafts Bund*, with the understanding that it function secretly. The list of members was to be controlled by Neumann.

Scharpp explained that secrecy was advisable to avoid antagonizing the Panamanian Government, "which is friendly to Italy and we can cooperate with the Italian Legation here."

"The Japanese are more important that the Italians," Kohpcke pointed out.

"The Japanese will work with us," Heildelk assured him.

"But we can't be seen with them—"

"Fritz [Kohpcke] will call a meeting in Jacobs' house," said Scharpp.

"Jacobs!" exclaimed one of the unidentified men. "You don't mean the Austrian Consul!"

Scharpp nodded slowly. "He is generally believed to be anti-Nazi. His partner spent twelve years in Japan and speaks Japanese perfectly. The Japanese Consul knows and trusts both. We cannot find a better place."

On the night of December 13, 1937, forty carefully selected Germans who, during the intervening month had become members of the Bund in Panama, arrived singly and in small groups at the home of August Jacobs-Kantstein, Panamanian merchant and Austrian Honorary Consul.

Five Japanese, headed by Tetsuo Umimoto, also came. One, K. Ishibashi, formerly captain of the "Hokkai Maru" and a reserve officer in the Japanese Navy; K. Ohihara, a Japanese agent staying with the

Japanese Consul but having no visible reason to be in Panama; two captains of Japanese fishing boats and A. Sonada, the barber who organized the labor union and in whose presence the Consul does not sit until the barber is seated.

Throughout the meeting, presided over by the elderly but tall and soldierly Austrian Consul, the Japanese said little. It was primarily the first get-together for Nazi-Japanese cooperation in the Canal Zone area.

"Mr. Umimoto has not said much," remarked Jacobs.

"There is so little to say when there are so many present," said the little Consul apologetically.

The others understood. The Japanese were too shrewd to discuss detailed plans with so many present.

A few days later Umimoto called upon Heildelk and was closeted with him for three hours. Shortly after that Sonada made a hurried trip to Japan.

VI SECRET AGENTS ARRIVE IN AMERICA

GERMANY'S INTEREST IN THE Panama Canal became acute only after Japan joined the Rome-Berlin axis "to exchange information about Communism"—an exchange which appears to be more concerned with military secrets than with Communism.

The activities of Japanese and Nazi agents in Latin American countries and especially around the Canal, the organizing of a fascist rebellion in Mexico to the south of us and intensive propaganda carried on in Canada to the north, are but part of the broad invasion of the Western Hemisphere by the Fifth Column—an invasion which began almost immediately after Hitler got into power. Since the United States is the most important country in the Americas, it was and is subject to special concentration by secret Nazi agents.

※ ※ ※

The first threads spun spread out in many directions, with propaganda as the base from which to broaden espionage activities. One of the earliest of the secret agents sent to this country was an American, Colonel Edwin Emerson, soldier of fortune, mediocre author and fairly competent war correspondent. Emerson lived at 215 East 15th Street, New York City and had an office in Room 1923 at 17 Battery Place, the address of the

German Consulate General. Room 1923 was rented by a representative of the German Consul General. The rent paid was nominal and in at least one instance, to avoid its being traced, it was paid in cash by Hitler's diplomatic representative. Prior to the renting of this room, Emerson had desk space with the German Consulate General for six weeks.

The May 15, 1933, issue of the *Amerika Deutsche Post,* a Nazi propaganda organ published in New York, carried an advertisement stating that the editor of this paper made his headquarters in Emerson's room. This was the first indication that Emerson had arrived in this country to handle Nazi propaganda.

For many years Emerson had wandered about the globe covering assignments for newspapers and magazines and always bragging about his Americanism and his "patriotism." One of his great boasts was that he was with Roosevelt's Rough Riders during the Spanish-American war; what he never told was that Roosevelt brought him back from Cuba in irons.

From his room paid for by the German Consul General, Emerson launched the "Friends of Germany."[6] This organization was the chief disseminator of pro-Hitler and anti-democratic propaganda in the United States, but the Colonel directed the propaganda somewhat stupidly. The "Friends of Germany" held meetings with "storm troops" in full uniform; bitter attacks were made against Jews and Catholics at large mass meetings. Visiting officers and sailors, from German ships docked in New York, appeared at these meetings to preach fascism and Nazism, until a wave of resentment swept the country. One of the keynotes of these talks was sounded by Edward F. Sullivan of Boston at a meeting held at Turnhalle, Lexington Avenue and 85th Street, on June 5th, 1934, when

---

6 Subsequently changed to "Friends of the New Germany" and then to the current "German-American Bund."

he repeatedly referred to Jews as "dirty, stinking kikes" and announced that he proposed to organize a strong Nazi group in Boston.

Propaganda Minister Goebbels in Berlin became annoyed at the public reaction, and the entire Nazi foreign propaganda service was reorganized. Emerson was ordered back to Germany for explicit instructions on how to carry on propaganda without antagonizing the entire country.

In October, 1933, Royal Scott Gulden (who has no connection with the mustard business, but is a distant relative of the head of it), who had been cooperating with Emerson, tried to organize an espionage system to watch Communists. In this effort Gulden enlisted the aid of Fred R. Marvin, a professional patriot. At three o'clock on the afternoon of March 10, 1934, a very secret meeting was called by Gulden at 139 East 57th Street. Present were Gulden, J. Schmidt and William Dudley Pelley, head of the Silver Shirts.

The meeting decided to adopt anti-semitic propaganda—to play on latent anti-semitism—as part of the first campaign to attract followers. The country was in a serious economic crisis with considerable unrest throughout the land. Both Hitler and Mussolini got into power in periods of great unrest by promising peace and security to the bewildered people. Men of means were terrified by fears of "revolution" and this group, directed by Emerson, began to preach that the revolution might come any minute and that the Jews were responsible for Moscow, the Third International, the Mississippi flood and anything else that troubled the people. When the meeting ended the "Order of '76"[7] had been born and Royal Scott Gulden appointed Secretary to direct espionage and propaganda.

---

7 Still functioning on a minor scale. The Fifth Column has since these early beginnings established much more efficient groups.

From the very beginning Emerson tried to get people into places which would provide access to important information. On February 22, 1934, a merger of the Republican Senatorial and Congressional Campaign Committees to conduct the Party's Congressional campaign independent of the Republican National Committee was announced in a joint statement by Senator Daniel O. Hastings of Delaware and Representative Chester C. Bolton of Ohio, chairmen, respectively, of the two committees.

Several weeks before this announcement, the two committees had employed Sidney Brooks, for years head of the research bureau of the International Telephone and Telegraph Company. Brooks, because of his position, was close in the confidences of Republican Senators and Congressmen. He heard state secrets and had his fingers on the political pulse of the country.

Shortly after he took charge of the joint committee for the Senators and Congressmen, Brooks made a hurried visit to New York. On March 4, 1934, he drove to the Hotel Edison and went directly to Room 830 where a man registered as "William D. Goodales—Los Angeles," was awaiting him. Mr. "Goodales" was William Dudley Pelley, head of the Silver Shirts, who had come to New York to confer with Brooks and Gulden. After this conference the two went to Gulden's office where they had a confidential talk that lasted over an hour during which an agreement was made to merge the Order of '76 with the Silver Shirts so as to carry on their propaganda more effectively.

Brooks himself, on his mysterious visits to New York, went to 17 Battery Place, which houses the German Consulate General. At that address he visited one John E. Kelly. In a letter to Kelly dated as far back as December 27, 1933, he wrote: "I will be in New York Friday to Monday and can be reached in the usual manner—Gramercy 5-9193 (care Emerson)."

*Application by Sidney Brooks for membership in the secret Order of '76,
showing him to be a son of the Nazi agent, Colonel Edwin Emerson.*

Sidney Brooks also was a member of the secret Order of '76. Before anyone could join he had to give, in his own handwriting and sealed with his own fingerprints, certain details of his life. Brooks' application for membership in this espionage group organized with the help of a Nazi sent to this country, revealed that he was the son of the Nazi agent, Colonel Edwin Emerson, and that he was using his mother's maiden name so that connection could not be traced too easily.

One of the other early propagandists who is still active as a "patriot" was Edward H. Hunter, Executive Secretary of the Industrial Defense Association, Inc., 7 Water Street, Boston. Early in 1934, while the negotiations for the merging of the espionage order and the Silver Shirts were going on, this rooter for American liberty heard Germany was spending money in this country and on March 3, he wrote to the "Friends of Germany":

> Under separate cover we are sending you twenty-five copies of our *Swan Song of Hate* as requested and you may have as many as you wish.

Several times I have conferred with Dr. Tippelskirch and at one time suggested that if he could secure the financial backing from Germany, I could start a real campaign along lines that would be very effective.

All that is necessary to return America to Americans is to organize the many thousands of persons who are victims of Judaism and I am ready to do that at any time.

Dr. Tippelskirch, with whom Hunter discussed getting money from Germany for anti-semitic work, was the German Consul in Boston.

* * *

The activities of the early agents ranged from propaganda to smuggling and espionage, though at the beginning the espionage was on a minor scale. It took several years of organizing pro-German groups in this country before they could pick the most reliable for the more dangerous spy work. Much of the propaganda was sent in openly through the mails, but some of it was of so vicious and anti-democratic character that the Propaganda Ministry in Germany decided it was wiser to smuggle it in from Nazi ships.

One of the chief smugglers was Guenther Orgell,[8] at that time head of the "Friends of Germany," through whom the propaganda was distributed to various branches of the organization throughout the country. In those days Orgell lived at 606 West 115th Street, New York City,[9] and was ostensibly employed as an electrical engineer by the Raymond Roth Co., 25 West 45th Street. Let me illustrate how he worked:

8 Following passage of the new 1938 law requiring all foreign agents to register, Orgell registered with the State Department as a German agent.

9 He now lives at Great Kills, Staten Island, N. Y.

At twenty minutes to ten on the evening of March 16, 1934, the North German Lloyd "Europa" was preparing to sail at midnight. The gaily illuminated boat was filled with men and women, many in evening dress, seeing friends off to Europe. German stewards, all of them members of the ship's Nazi *Gruppe,* stood about smiling, bowing, but watching every passenger and visitor carefully.

People wandered all over the boat. Many visited the library on the main promenade deck, which has a German post office. There was a great deal of laughter and chatter. Orgell, dressed in an ordinary business suit and carrying a folded newspaper in his hands, wandered in. Catching the post office steward's eye, he casually took four letters from his coat pocket and handed them to the steward who as casually slipped them into his pocket. There were no stamps on the letters, which, incidentally, constituted a federal offense.

Still so casual in manner that the average observer would not even have noticed the transfer of the letters, Orgell wandered over to a desk in the library and rapidly wrote another letter—so important, apparently, that he dared not carry it with him for fear of a mishap. The letter was sealed and handed to the steward.

The library had a great many visitors. No one seemed to be paying any attention to this visitor or passenger talking to the steward. With a quick glance around him, Orgell took in everyone in the library and seemed satisfied. He caught the steward's eye again and nodded. The steward opened a closet in the library, the second one left of the main aisle on the port side toward the stern of the boat. A thin package was taken from its hiding place and quickly slipped to Orgell who covered it with his newspaper and promptly left the ship.

This was the manner in which Nazi secret instructions and spy reports were sent and received—a procedure that kept up until the arrest of the Nazi spies who were tried late in 1938.

When Orgell needed trusted men to deliver messages to and from the boats as well as to smuggle off material, he usually called upon the American branch of the *Stahlhelm,* or Steel Helmets, which used to drill secretly in anticipation of *Der Tag* in this country. Only when he felt that he was not being watched, or only in the event of the most important messages, did he go aboard the ships personally. Orgell's liaison man in the smuggling activities was Frank Mutschinski, a painting contractor who used to live at 116 Garland Court, Garritsen Beach, N.Y.

Mutschinski came to the United States from Germany on the S.S. "George Washington," June 16, 1920. He was commander of one of the American branches of the *Stahlhelm* which had offices at 174 East 85th Street, New York. While he was in command, he received his orders direct from Franz Seldte, subsequently Minister of Labor under Hitler. Seldte at that time was in Magdeburg, Germany. Branches of the *Stahlhelm* were established by him and Orgell in Rochester, Chicago, Philadelphia, Newark, Detroit, Los Angeles and Toronto (the first step in the Fifth Column's invasion of Canada).

To help Orgell in his smuggling activities, Mutschinski supplied him with a chief assistant, Carl Brunkhorst. It was Brunkhorst's job to deliver the secret letters. Nazi uniforms for American Storm Troopers were smuggled into this country off German ships by Paul Bante who lived at 186 East 93rd Street, New York City. Bante, at the time he was engaged in the smuggling activities, was a member of the 244th Coast Guard as well as the New York National Guard.

In the early days of organizing the Nazi web over the United States, the German agents received cooperation from racketeering "patriots" who saw possibilities of scaring the wits out of the American people by announcing that the "revolution" was just around the corner. The country was in an economic crisis, the American people were bewildered and didn't know which way to turn, there was considerable unrest in the land, and the Nazi agents and their American counterparts visualized in Hitler's cry that "Communism and the Jews" were responsible, grand pickings from the scared suckers.

Since Communism, especially in those restless days in the depths of the depression, was the bugaboo of the rich, it was inevitable that some unscrupulous but shrewd observers of the American scene would take advantage of this fear and capitalize on it. One of the chief racketeers, a man who subsequently worked very closely with secret Nazi agents in this country, was Harry A. Jung, Honorary General Manager of the American Vigilant Intelligence Federation, Post Office Box 144, Chicago. This organization was originally founded to spy on Communists and Socialists. For a while Jung collected from terrified employers by promising to inform them about the threat of revolution—what time it would occur and who would lead it. In return he collected plenty.

In time employers got fed up when the rowboat loaded with bomb-throwing Bolsheviks failed to arrive from Moscow. Pickings became slim. Jung was badly in need of a new terror-inspiring "issue" with which to collect from the suckers. He found it at the time Emerson was sent here from Germany. Gulden, Pelley and their associates were launching an anti-semitic campaign as the first step to attract people to the "Friends of Germany." Jung likewise discovered the "menace of the Jew" and peddled it for all it was worth.

There was an air of secrecy about the whole outfit. Even the location of the office in the Chicago Tribune Tower was kept from the membership; all they were given was the post office box number. As soon as he collected enough material from the *Daily Worker* and other Communist publications, he sent agents to call on the gullible businessmen with

Showing the type of literature peddled by patrioteer Harry A. Jung.

horrendous stories of the Muscovites now on the high seas on their way to capture the American Government. The salesmen collected and in turn got forty per cent of the pickings.

When Jung heard that William Dudley Pelley was making money on the Jew-and-Catholic scare and that others like Edward H. Hunter of the Industrial Defense Association were talking with the German Consul General about getting money from Germany for propaganda, he got busy peddling "The Protocols of the Elders of Zion," long discredited as forgeries. Armed with these, Jung's high pressure salesmen scoured the country, collecting shekels from Christian businessmen and getting their forty per cent commissions.

It was not long before Jung, Pelley and others were working in full swing with secret Nazi agents sent into this country for propaganda and espionage purposes.

VII NAZI SPIES AND AMERICAN "PATRIOTS"

ONCE THE SPADEWORK WAS done by the early Nazi agents sent into the United States, the web rapidly embraced native fascists, racketeering "patriots" and deluded Americans who swallowed their propaganda. When Japan joined the Rome-Berlin axis, espionage directed against American naval and military forces became one of the major interests of the foreign agents, especially on the West Coast.

Some five years ago, after the McCormick Congressional Committee investigation into Nazi activities turned up a number of propagandists, there was a lull in their activity until the nationwide denunciations died out. In the meantime Goebbels again ordered the reorganization of the entire propaganda machine in this country.

It was during this period that the approaching Presidential elections presented an immediate task for the Nazis to work on. The Roosevelt Administration was considered by the Nazis both here and in Germany as none too friendly to Hitler, and before the election got well under way the Nazis here, upon instructions from their local leaders who act only upon instructions from the German Propaganda Bureau, became active in the anti-Roosevelt campaign. Both Nazi agents and "patriotic" American groups working with Nazi agents (without much money after the Congressional Committee's exposés) suddenly found themselves possessed of more than enough capital with which to

MENE, MENE, TEKEL, UPSHARON

THE JEW IS OUR SOCIAL PERIL

GET RID OF ROOSEVELT
AND HIS JEWS

ELIMINATE JEWS FROM PUBLIC OFFICE

SMASH JEW-DOMINATION OF
W.P.A. and S.R.A.

AND ALL STATE AND COUNTY CHARITY RELIEF

Read and study the Protocols of the Elders of Zion.
An Exposure of Jew-Communist Conspiracy.

For Information, Address The American White Guard P. O. Box 1 East Pasadena. California.

American White Guard Press Chicago, Ill.

Anti-Semitic anti-Roosevelt handbill issued by
the American White Guard in California.

operate. Some of the money came from the Nazis and some from anti-Roosevelt forces.

One of the most vicious of the anti-Roosevelt propaganda mediums was established by Nazi agents in a carefully hidden printing plant.

No one who got off on the sixth floor at 325 W. Ohio St., Chicago, and entered the John Baumgarth's Specialty Company, would have suspected anything out of the ordinary about the place. It looked just like hundreds of other business firms where pale girls and anemic-looking men made calendars.

People came up on the ancient elevator, attended to their affairs at the desks in front of the door, and left. Very few of them ever went behind the enormous piles of cardboard and paper which almost obstructed the passage to the right of the desks. But if you turned into this passage and then turned to the left, you came upon a wooden partition. Unless you were watching for it you would think it a wall.

There was no indication of what was behind the partition. There was only a shiny Yale lock in a door carefully hidden from the eyes of casual visitors. If you knew nothing about it and tried to open the the door, you would find it locked. If you knocked or banged on it, there would be no answering sign from the other side, and the young man operating the cutting machine alongside the partition would merely stare at you blankly.

But if you knocked three times quickly, paused for a split second and then knocked once more, the door would be opened immediately. Without the proper signal all the knocking in the world would not help, for this was the entrance to the carefully guarded publication rooms of the *American Gentile* and the headquarters for Nazi anti-democratic activities in the Middle West. But even more guarded than the location of the printing plant were the goings and comings of the paper's editor, Captain Victor DeKayville and his financial backer, Charles O'Brien.

This brings me to two of the leading Nazi agents in the United States, one of whom originally started the newspaper. Certainly none of the American suckers who gave them money to spread pro-Nazi propaganda knew that both were masquerading under false names and that one of them is an ex-convict.

※　※　※

Those social leaders in Chicago and San Francisco, whose doors were always open to the handsome, dashing Prince Peter Kushubue with his sad eyes and his talk of how the Bolsheviki had confiscated his vast estates and family jewels in Old Russia, may be interested to learn that his Highness, the Prince, is really—well, let me give a brief sketch of his activities before he became a Nazi agent:

In 1922, a Russian emigré, born in Petrograd and christened Peter Afanassieff or Aphanassieff, came to the United States seeking his fortune, preferably in the form of a wealthy heiress. As an ordinary run-of-the-mill Afanassieff, he was just an unemployed White Russian looking for a job and it didn't take him long to discover that in this democratic country heiresses and their doting papas go nuts over titles. So overnight Peter Afanassieff blossomed out into Prince Peter Kushubue; and as a Prince whose wealth had been confiscated by the Bolsheviki, the doors of San Francisco society opened to him.

Afanassieff just barely missed marrying a wealthy heiress on the West Coast, and in his despondence he tried his hand at a little forgery. But he picked the wrong outfit to practice penmanship on. He forged a United States Treasury check and when the federal men got after him he fled to Chicago. He was picked up and on November 29, 1929, he found himself before a U.S. Commissioner who ordered his return to San Francisco. On December 19 of the same year he pleaded guilty before Federal Judge F. J. Kerrigan and was given a year and a half. At the trial he admitted to being just an ordinary Afanassieff and served his sentence under that name.

When he came out he alternated between being Prince Kushubue and an ordinary Afanassieff and then, because the 1930 crash had kicked the bottom out of the market for foreign titles, he picked himself a good solid American name: Armstrong. He said it was his mother's maiden name. For convenience we'll call him Armstrong from now on.

When he arrived in Chicago in 1933, he met some White Russians who were working with Harry A. Jung on an altogether new translation of the "Protocols." Jung planned to publish and distribute the forgeries in order to scare the wits out of his Christian suckers, but changed his mind when he discovered he could buy them cheaper and resell at a higher price. Jung, in turn, introduced Armstrong to Nazi agents.

Jung and the ex-convict hit it up. Before long Armstrong became Jung's secret agent No. 31 (Jung is No. 1 and always signs his letters to agents with that number. His agents, too, sign only their numbers. They are not sup-posed even to write the number but every once in a while an agent slips up and scribbles a postscript in his own handwriting. A reproduction of one of No. 31's reports to the No. 1 Guy appears on the opposite page.)

It was not long after Jung introduced Armstrong to Nazi agents that the White Russian decided that he could work the racket himself. He began to meet secretly with Nazi agents without telling Jung about it. Their favorite meeting place was at Von Thenen's Tavern, 2357 Roscoe St., Chicago. Present at these meetings, usually called by Fritz Gissibl, head of the "Friends of the New Germany,"[10] were Armstrong, Captain Victor DeKayville, J. K. Leibl (who organized an underground Nazi clique in South Bend, Ind.), Oscar Pfaus, Nick Mueller, Toni Mueller, Jose Martini, Franz Schaeffer and Gregor Buss. When Gissibl couldn't attend, his right-hand man Leibl acted for him.

In March, 1936, Armstrong and the others decided to establish a "National Alliance" to aid in Nazi work. They decided to use the utmost secrecy lest what they were doing and who were behind it, leak out. They met only in private homes and so careful were they that the host of one meeting would not be told where the next meeting was to be held. Only a picked handful of the most trusted Nazi agents were invited.

The first meeting was held at Bockhold's home, 1235 Waveland Ave., Chicago; the second at the home of Mrs. Emma Schmid, 4710 Winthrop Ave., Chicago. To the second meeting they invited C. O. Anderson of 601 Diversey Parkway, Chicago. He was listed by the Nazis and the White Russians as a good sucker because he had contributed money to Jung.

The White Russians and the Nazi agents then decided to start a publishing business as the first step to attract followers. They issued

---

10 Gissibl left for Stuttgart, Germany, and leadership was taken over by his brother, Peter.

Grand Rapids Michigan.

Dear # 1.

Yours of Twelvth instant received and Mr.Shere delivered your packag to me last Saturday.

Refering to my of II/inst.I was able to acomplish only part of a job.Mr.Thompson and Mr.Tolliefiere were out of townso I'll try to get in tuch with both on Monday. Saturday a.m.I had one hour and 20m.talk with editor of G.R.Herald Mr.Frank Sparks. He read my credentials and after coversing a while we agreed upon that something should be done and done in a hurry.I left with that chap our 3 documents(legal size), memo on Foster ,A.V.I.F. programme/blue/C.P.U.S.A.chart,Facing the facts and Vigilant. I think it will be good idea if you send him afew lines mentioning how glad you are o.t.c.Same evening I received invitation to attend diner at Dr.Ferris N.Smith (659 Ply-mouth blvd.Grand Rapids,Mich.)He is a very prominent ,rich and internationaly known Plastic Surgery cpesialist.In my honour we had 2 bottles of champaign and other things beside.Diner party ended at 4.30 a.m.Sunday.Most interesting part of it that Mrs.Smith just few weeks ago came back from U.S.S.R.where she spend 10 days in Moscow.She is very wellversed in Bolshevik end of our problems But also very much like to find outother "WHY-S?".So last nite she pledged herself to A.V.I.F.and wills sighn card on my return back to Grand Rapids.Mr.Gerry D.Pettibone of 206 Lafayette Ave.N.E.-signed card last Tuesday but did not paid money-will Collect later.

Fpeaking of #679 according to opinion of Dr.S.G.he lakes backbone as an organizer, altnee remember that I am Quoting some one elsie opinion.I can not have of my own in this case 'cose I saw him so little.

Tomorrow I'll try to see Tolliefiere and also Thompson.Then in an Evening to see] again Dr. F.N.Smith.

Yours &тr

Enclos.

*"P.S Tuesday leaving for Detroit,
ill stay with Dr. at Tuller Hotel.*

*Letter written by secret agent No. 31 (Peter Afanassieff, alias
Prince Kushubue, alias Peter V. Armstrong) to No. 1 (Harry A. Jung).*

Nibelungen-Verlag G.m.b.H.

Berlin NW 40, In den Zelten 9a

Auslieferungsstelle nur Leipzig C 1, Täubchenweg 17
Fernruf: Berlin A 1 Jäger-5644, Leipzig 71244
Postscheckkonto: Berlin 78302
Bankkonto: Deutsche Bank und Disconto-Gesellschaft, Depositenkasse S 2,
Berlin NW 40, Alt-Moabit 109

Herrn
Peter V. Armstrong
i.Fa. Patriotic Publishing Co.
C h i c a g o .

Dear Sir,
By Mr. Lilienfeld we were informed that you are interested in
the english edition of our book: Herman Fehst, Bolschewism and
Jewry. We beg to inform you that the right of edition of this
...k and all

a   ..t in au arice
later on we will deduct the sale every half a year.

We await with interest your answer.

Yours faithfully
Nibelungen-Verlag
G. m. b. H.

*Letter showing contact between Peter V. Armstrong (the White Russian
ex-convict Peter Afanassieff) and German publishers of anti-Semitic literature.*

a paper called the *Gentile Front*. They were extremely careful to keep
the editorial and publication addresses secret. All mail was sent only
to Post Office Box No. 526 in the old Chicago Post Office. The company
was named the Patriotic Publishing Co. and with the utmost secrecy
editorial offices were established at 5 S. Wabash in Chicago and the
paper printed in the basement at 4233 N. Kildare where the Merrimac
Press functioned.

Subsequently, to throw anyone who might be watching them off the
trail, they changed the name of the publishing company to the Right

Cause Publishing Co. and issued an avalanche of Nazi propaganda. It was through this secretly organized and secretly functioning propaganda center that Harry A. Jung, ultra-"patriot," distributed printed attacks on Roosevelt just before the Presidential election.

❦ ❦ ❦

The *American Gentile,* backed by Nazi money, published the most insane rantings imaginable. But when one is inclined to dismiss them as insanity, one remembers that it was the same sort of stuff Hitler used in winning millions of bewildered Germans to his banner. The pre-election issue (October, 1936) of the *Gentile* will serve as an illustration of what they published and distributed through the United States mails:

Former Congressman Louis T. McFadden[11] died on October 1 from a stroke. He was sixty years old. The *American Gentile,* however, implied that he had been murdered by Jews; Senator Bronson Cutting (killed in an airplane crash) also was murdered by Jews. Huey Long was murdered by Jews. Walter A. Liggett, the newspaper editor, was murdered by Jews, and it was an international ring of Jewish bankers who hired Booth to murder Abraham Lincoln.

Of course it was crazy, but the coal digger in Kentucky or the bedeviled farmer in the Middle West who couldn't pay his taxes or the unemployed worker in an industrial center who couldn't find a job did not know history any too well nor understand the workings of the economic system; and when they were told by newspapers brought to them by the United States Government mails that their economic difficulties were due to a Jewish-Communist plot, that Roosevelt was a Jew

11 Before McFadden died, I published evidence that while he was a member of Congress he worked with Nazi agents in this country.

and was controlled by Jews and Communists, some of them were prone to believe it. With this irresponsible propaganda anti-semitism grew. Men and women were attracted to the Nazi web without dreaming of the forces disseminating the propaganda of the motives behind them.

※ ※ ※

The most capable of those drawn into the Nazi propaganda machine were chosen for more serious work. Some were used for propaganda; others were given definite espionage assignments. The espionage and propaganda divisions of the Nazi machine in this country are separate bodies. They overlap only in serving as a recruiting ground.

The smuggling of anti-democratic propaganda off Nazi ships entering American ports was exposed by the McCormick Congressional Committee, but it stopped only for a brief period. The Nazi ships which bring in propaganda also bring secret instructions to agents here and take back their reports. To eliminate tell-tale evidence, Dr. George Gyssling, Nazi Consul in Los Angeles, has paid out cash to leaders of the German propaganda machine on the West Coast. Affidavits to this effect are in my possession.

The headquarters for the West Coast propaganda machine which dabbles a little in espionage, is the *Deutsches Haus,* 634 W. 15th Street, Los Angeles. The building is supposed to be merely a meeting place for German-Americans and sympathizers of the Hitler regime. Actually its functions are far more sinister.

The *Deutsches Haus,* before it was turned into a center of Nazi activity, had been a typical Los Angeles home. When the Nazis took it over, they ripped out several of the front rooms and turned it into a barn-like affair with a skylight overhead and a raised platform from which speakers sing the praises of Hitler and fascism. In the rear part of the hall is a combined bar and restaurant where the German-Americans drink their beer and whiskies and plot the smuggling of propaganda from Nazi ships and the carrying on of espionage against American military and naval forces.

I use the word "plot" for precisely what it means. From this house, naturalized American citizens and native Americans direct espionage and propaganda activities paid for by a foreign government and designed against the peace and security of the United States.

The leader of this group, Hermann Schwinn, was appointed by Minister of Propaganda Goebbels in Germany and is the recipient of personal letters of praise from Adolf Hitler for his work. Schwinn is a naturalized citizen,[12] a comparatively young man in his early thirties, ruddy-faced and with a thin, quivering mustache on his upper lip. This little Führer's office is just off the meeting hall and adjoins the small bookstore where the purchaser can get pamphlets, books, and newspapers attacking democracy.

When I called upon Schwinn at the Nazi headquarters and introduced myself, he smiled amiably and granted my request for an interview. The German-American Bund, he explained immediately (the reorganized Friends of the New Germany), is now a patriotic organization, consisting only of American citizens.

The German-American Bund, Schwinn continued as we seated ourselves in his office, was now a "patriotic organization striving to create among Americans a better understanding of Nazi Germany, to combat anti-Nazi propaganda and the boycott against Germany, and to fight Communism." He took about ten minutes to explain their peaceful objectives and their great love for the United States.

---

12 As this book went to press, the U. S. Government had just begun action to revoke Schwinn's citizenship, claiming that he had obtained it by making false statements.

"Everything is America for the Americans and to fight all alien theories and interests?" I asked, summing up his explanation.

"That's right," he beamed.

"Does any propaganda come from Germany to help save America for the Americans?"

"No, sir!" he said. "We have nothing to do with Germany; we are Americans first. Mr. Dickstein[13] says that there is propaganda coming, but he was never able to prove any of his statements."

"Then how does propaganda like *World Service* from Erfurt, Germany, get into this country?"

"Oh, I get it," he said casually. "Anyone can subscribe to it for a dollar and a half a year. We get two or three copies around here—by subscription, of course."

"There must be a lot of subscribers in the United States for I've seen a great many copies. I thought that perhaps it comes in batches from Germany for distribution here so members of the Nazi groups in the United States could use it to help save America for the Americans."

"No," he smiled. "It's all a subscription matter."

"I see. Do you know Captain George Trauernicht?"

Schwinn shot a startled glance at me and nodded slowly. "Yes," he said, "he's Captain of the Hapag Line ship 'Oakland.'"

"Do you ever visit him?"

"Yes; he was here last week."

"Doesn't he bring batches of *World Service* and other propaganda for you every time he comes into port?"

"No," Schwinn said sharply. "The visits I pay him are purely social. Just to drink a glass of good German beer."

---

13 Congressman Samuel Dickstein. The McCormick Congressional Committee was frequently referred to as the "Dickstein Committee" because Dickstein had introduced the resolution for the investigation.

"Do you usually pay social visits carrying a brief case?"

"Now, wait a minute," he protested. "Don't write down the answer until I think."

I stopped typing on his office machine which he had permitted me to use to take verbatim notes of the interview and waited while he thought. After a lengthy silence I added:

"You had a brief case on Thursday when you visited him."

He continued thinking for a little longer and then said that he thought he had had a brief case on that trip.

"But why do you ask me that?" he demanded. "There was nothing in that brief case."

"Sure there was. The brief case always contains reports you send back to Germany and instructions from Germany are brought to you by Captain Trauernicht as well as other captains of German ships docking here and in San Diego."

"I have never taken off propaganda nor given nor received reports," Schwinn insisted. "Somebody told you something and you've got it all wrong."

"Suppose I mention a few instances. At four o'clock on Monday afternoon, March 9, 1936, your beer-drinking friend, Captain Trauernicht, waited for you at the gangplank of his boat—for your 'social' visit. What he wanted was the package of sealed reports from Nazi agents throughout the United States which you were bringing in your brief case. In due time you arrived and gave him the reports. Then you started on a drinking spree—"

"I don't know what you're talking about," Schwinn interrupted.

"Maybe I can refresh your memory. That was the evening the Captain took a lady from Beverly Hills, to the first mate's cabin—remember? You know, the lady who lives on North Crescent Drive—shall I mention her name?"

Schwinn's face turned an apoplectic red and he became quiet.

"On Monday, February 10, 1936," I continued. "Reinhold Kusche, leader of the O. D. unit in your organization and a 'patriotic' naturalized American citizen, was on board the steamer 'Elbe' docked in Los Angeles harbor. He telephoned to one of your Nazi agents, Albert Voigt, that the Captain was sailing at five o'clock for Antwerp and was furious because the agents' reports had not yet been delivered to him. Kusche told Voigt to bring the reports in a hurry—which Voigt promptly did.

"On Tuesday evening, May 12, 1936, the Captain of the Nazi ship 'Schwaben', which had just arrived from Antwerp, Belgium, came to your office and handed you a sealed package of orders and propaganda. He laid it on your desk in this room. The package contained copies of *World Service*—which is obtainable, you remember, only by subscription at a dollar and a half a year."

"It is not true—" Schwinn interrupted excitedly.

"I have a copy from the batch he brought to you. But let's continue. On Monday, June 8, 1936, you yourself went to the Nazi ship 'Weser' and gave the captain secret reports to take back to Germany and left with secret orders he had brought over—orders sealed in brown, manila paper[14]—and a large package of *Fichte-Bund* propaganda. I have a copy from that batch, too."

Schwinn stared at me and then smiled. "You can't prove anything," he said with assurance.

"I have affidavits about all these items and more—affidavits from men on board the Nazi ships."

"It's impossible!" he exclaimed. "No German on the ship would dare to sign an affidavit!"

---

14 During the trial of the four Nazi spies in New York the Federal prosecutor brought out that they also carried orders sealed in brown, manila paper.

"But I have them," I repeated.

"You intend to publish them?" he asked, a cunning look appearing in his eyes.

His eagerness to discover who had given me affidavits was funny and I laughed. "I'll publish the information contained in them," I explained. "The names of the signers will be given only to an American governmental or judicial body which may look into your 'patriotic' activities. But let's get on. Do you know the Nazi Consul in Los Angeles—Dr. George Gyssling?"

He sat silently for a moment as if hesitating whether to speak.

"Don't be afraid to talk," I said. "The Consul isn't. You know, of course, that he does not like you?"

A deep red flush suffused his face. "It's mutual!" he said. "I know he talks—"

Throughout the interview Schwinn tried almost pathetically, despite his obvious dislike of Gyssling, to cover up the Consul's interference in American affairs. When I told Schwinn I had affidavits showing that Rafael Demmler, President of the Steuben Society of Los Angeles, got two hundred dollars in April, 1936, from the Nazi Consul to help maintain the *Deutsches Haus* as a center of Nazi propaganda, he shook his head bewilderedly; and when I pointed out that he himself got one hundred and forty-five dollars in cash from the Nazi Consul on Tuesday, April 28, 1936, to cover expenses incurred by Schwinn in the effort to bring the German-American groups together for the better dissemination of Nazi propaganda, his face turned alternately white and red and finally he exploded:

"Did Gyssling tell you that?"

"I'm not saying who told it to me. But let's get on with some of your other 'patriotic' activities. On Thursday, June 18, 1936, you visited Captain Trauernicht in company with Count von Bülow—"

For the first time since the interview began Schwinn sat upright in his chair as if I had struck him. All the other subjects had left him slightly disturbed but still with an obvious sense that he was not on particularly dangerous ground. But at the mention of Von Bülow's name a look of actual fear spread over his face.

"On that day," I continued, "you and the Count went directly to the Captain's cabin where you handed over your reports—"

"What are you getting at?" Schwinn demanded sharply.

"I'm getting at the Count. What do you know about him?"

"Nothing. I know nothing about him. I've met him, that's all."

"Have you ever visited his home at Point Loma,[15] San Diego?"

Schwinn stared at me without answering.

"Have you ever been there?" I repeated.

"Yes," he said slowly.

"Did you ever observe how, through his study windows, you could see almost everything going on at the American naval base—"

"I have nothing to say," Schwinn interrupted excitedly.

Among the men sent here directly by Rudolf Hess, Hitler's right-hand man, is a former German-American businessman named Meyer-hofer. This Nazi came here with special instructions from Hess, a personal friend of his, to reorganize the Nazi machine in the United States. He arrived early in 1935 posing as a businessman. After consultations with Nazi leaders in New York, including the Nazi Consul General, he went to Detroit to confer with Fritz Kuhn,[16] national head of the German-American Bund. From Detroit he went to Chicago where he held more conferences with Nazi agents and then went directly to Los Angeles for conferences with Schwinn, Von Bülow and other

15 Von Bülow has since sold his home and moved into the El Cortez Hotel in San Diego.

16 At that time working for Henry Ford.

secret agents operating in the United States. Meyerhofer's mission was not only to reorganize the propaganda machine but to try to place it on a self-supporting basis so that in the event of war when funds from Germany would be cut off, an efficient Nazi machine could continue functioning.

It was with this knowledge in mind that I asked Schwinn what he knew about Meyerhofer. At the mention of his name the Nazi leader for the West Coast again showed a flash of fear. He hesitated a little longer than usual and then said in a low voice, "He is a member of our organization. He came from Germany about thirty or forty years ago." Suddenly he added, "He's an American citizen."

"I know he's an American citizen. But are you sure he didn't come from Germany—on his latest trip—in January of last year?"

Schwinn smiled a little wryly. "He might have," he said in the same low tone.

"He's a personal friend of Rudolf Hess—"

"Listen!" Schwinn exclaimed. "You're on the wrong track!"

"Maybe; but what's his business here?"

"He's a businessman!"

"What's his business?"

Schwinn shrugged his shoulders. "I don't know," he said and then with growing excitement, "I tell you you're on the wrong track!"

"Then what are you so excited about?"

"Because you're on the wrong track—"

"Okay. I'm on the wrong track and you know nothing about Nazi spies. Do you know of the visits paid by the Japanese Consul in Los Angeles to Nazi ships when they come into port and of his conferences with Nazi captains—"

"The Japanese! We have nothing to do with the Japanese. We are a patriotic group—"

"Yes, I know. What do you know about Schneeberger?"

Schwinn answered with an "M-m-m-m." His jaw bones showed against the ruddy flesh of his cheeks. He stared up at the ceiling. "He was a Tyrolian peasant boy," he said without looking at me. "A boy traveling around the world; you know, just chiseling his way around—"

"Just a bum, eh?"

"That's it," he agreed quickly. "Just a bum."

"What would your connections be with bums? Do you usually associate with Tyrolian bums who are chiseling their way around the world?"

"Oh, he just came here like so many other people. He wanted money; so I gave him a little help and he went to San Francisco and Oakland. He vanished. I haven't any idea where he might be now. Maybe he's in Chicago now."

"He couldn't possibly be in Japan now, could he?"

"He spoke of going to Japan," Schwinn admitted.

"You saw him off on a Japanese training ship which the Japanese Government sent here from the Canal Zone, didn't you?"

"I don't know," he said defiantly. "I know nothing about him."

"The treaty between Japan and Germany providing for exchange of information about Communists was signed November 25, 1936. But in September, 1936, Schneeberger told you he was leaving on a Japanese training ship for Japan. No training ship was expected on the West Coast at that time by the United States port authorities, and yet a Japanese training ship appeared—ordered here from the Canal Zone. It was on this ship that Schneeberger left. Apparently, then, the Nazis and the Japanese had already been working together—and you were cooperating because you took Schneeberger around. You took him to Count von Bülow's home at Point Loma, overlooking the American naval base. You know that Schneeberger was not broke because he was spending money freely—"

"He was broke," Schwinn interrupted weakly.

"If he was so broke, how do you account for his carrying around an expensive camera and always having plenty of film with which to photograph American naval and military spots?"

"I don't know. Maybe he carried the camera around to hock in case he went broke."

The absurdity of the excuse was so patent that I laughed. Schwinn smiled a little.

"All right. What do you know about a man named Maeder?"

Again that long, drawn-out "M-m-m-m." A long pause and Schwinn said, "Maeder is an American citizen, I believe."

"Yes; you are, too. But what's his business in this country?"

"I don't know," Schwinn said helplessly. "I really don't know."

"You know nothing about his activities or observations of American naval and military bases? Do you usually take in members without knowing anything about them?"

"Sometimes we do and sometimes we do not—"

"But orders were sent from Germany to make this an American organization—"

Schwinn nodded without admitting it verbally.

"And since you throw out all Germans who are not American citizens, you check with the Consul General in New York as to whether they are fit—"

"We have nothing to do with the Consul General—"

"What happened to Willi Sachse who used to be a member here?"

"He is supposed to have gone back to Germany."

"Have you heard from him from Germany?"

"No; I haven't heard since he left."

"You received a letter recently from him from San Francisco where he is watching foreign vessels—"

"Oh," said Schwinn, raising his hands in a helpless gesture, "I know you have spies in my organization."

We talked a little longer—of visits he made to Nazi agents in the Middle West and in New York, of secret conferences with propagandists and spies. But he refused to do any more than shrug his shoulders at all new questions.

"I have said too much already," he said.

VIII HENRY FORD AND SECRET NAZI ACTIVITIES

ONE OF THE CHIEF NAZI propagandists in the United States recently ran in the United States Senate primaries in Kansas and was almost nominated. He is Gerald B. Winrod, who poses as a Protestant minister but has no affiliations with any reputable church.

Winrod, even before he tried to get into the Senate, was one of the most brazen of the Nazis' Fifth Column operating in this country. He has held secret consultations with officials in the German Embassy in Washington and carries on his propaganda under Fritz Kuhn's direction.

Shortly after Winrod returned from a mysterious trip to Germany and held an equally mysterious long consultation at the Nazi Embassy in this country (1935), he organized the *Capitol News and Feature Service*, with offices at 209 Kellogg Building, Washington. The "news service" supplied smaller papers throughout the land with "impartial comments" on the national scene. The *Service* was edited by Dan Gilbert, a San Diego newspaperman, and the material was sent free of charge (as is the material sent to the Latin American countries from Germany and Italy). It was of course, deliberately calculated to spread pro-Hitler sentiment and propaganda.

Few who read Winrod's publications realize the extent of his activities. On March 1, 1937, Senator Joseph T. Robinson addressed the United

States Senate on what appeared to him to be "unfair propaganda" carried on by Winrod against President Roosevelt's proposed reorganization of the judiciary system. The Senator stated that he could not understand why the issues should be deliberately falsified by a gentleman of the cloth—that it reminded him of the old Ku Klux Klan tactics.

The Senator did not know that Winrod's propaganda against Roosevelt was only part of a propaganda campaign cunningly and brazenly organized by Nazis in this country in an effort to defeat a man who, they felt, was not friendly to them. In this campaign, Nazi agents worked openly and secretly with a few unscrupulous members of the Republican Party in an effort to defeat Roosevelt.

Several years ago Winrod was a poverty-stricken man living at 145 N. Green Street, Wichita, Kansas. He called himself a minister but all church bodies have repudiated him. Without a church, he did a little evangelistic preaching and lived off collections made from his audience. It was a precarious livelihood and often the "Reverend" did not have enough money to buy even ordinary necessities.

Records in several Wichita department stores tell the story of the evangelist's poverty before an angel came to visit him. All the storekeepers with whom Winrod dealt requested that their names be withheld, but signified their willingness to present their records to any governmental body which might be interested in the sudden wealth he acquired after he became an intense Hitler propagandist. In the days of his poverty Winrod, the records show, could afford to buy only the cheapest furniture, the cheapest clothes, and pay for them on the installment plan in weekly payments ranging from fifty cents to two or three dollars a week.

I am reproducing with this chapter several of the installment cards. The reader will notice that as late as 1934 Winrod was paying at the rate of one dollar a week. It was in this period that Nazi agents in the United

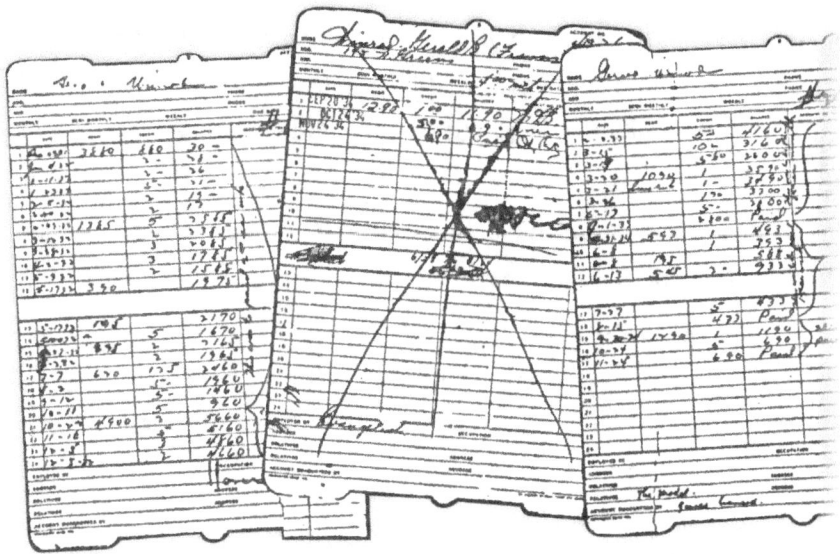

*Account cards for the Reverend Gerald B. Winrod in a Wichita department
store, showing his straitened financial circumstances during the early thirties.*

States were carrying on their intensive campaign, and it was also in this
period that Winrod began to harangue his audiences about the "menace of the Jews and the Catholics."

Then one day, the Reverend Gerald B. Winrod suddenly found
himself possessed of enough money to go to Germany. When he came
back in February, 1935, he had new suit cases, new clothes and a fat
check book. The records in the Wichita department stores where he
had been getting credit for clothes and furniture show that after his
return from Germany he paid all his debts in lump sums—by check.
Then he became a publisher.

In his newspaper, *The Revealer,* he published a report on his trip to
Europe, but did not mention where he got the money for the jaunt. The
report (February 15, 1935) told of his discovery that the German people
loved Hitler and that only "Jewish influence in high circles of certain
governments is making it impossible for Germany to carry on normal
trade and financial relations with other countries."

In this period of his new-found prosperity he established contacts with Nazi agents and pro-fascists like Harry A. Jung of the American Vigilant Intelligence Federation, Colonel Edwin Emerson, James True and a host of other patrioteers.

Before the Presidential election he made another trip to Germany. When he returned, he enlarged his distribution apparatus and was apparently important enough for high Nazi officials visiting the United States to meet with him. One of these was Hans von Reitenkranz, who came quietly to the United States as Hitler's personal representative to arrange for oil purchases—oil which Germany needed badly for her factories and especially for her growing war machine.

Von Reitenkranz is a friend of Professor Kurt Sepmeier of the University of Wichita. He introduced Winrod to the Professor. They became friendly. When I was in Wichita making inquiries about the Reverend Winrod, I constantly came across the Professor's trail. Both he and Winrod had been meeting regularly but with an effort at secrecy.

In January, 1937, after several meetings with Professor Sepmeier, Winrod went to Washington. I also went to Washington and found that the Reverend was calling at the German Embassy. On one of his visits he remained inside for an hour and eighteen minutes. Whom he saw or what he discussed I do not know; but immediately after this long visit, the *News and Feature Service* was organized with money enough to send its items out free of charge to the papers that would accept them.

Gilbert, who headed the *Service,* was for many years the personal representative of William Dudley Pelley, leader of the Silver Shirts. The Nazis had been trying to get the Silver Shirts to cooperate with them in a fascist "united front" and the appointment of Gilbert was the first indication that a friendly cooperation had been established.

Winrod had been in constant communication with Pelley, and Pelley had conferred several times with Schwinn. The Nazis were eager to

Sample of the "Capital News and Feature Service," in the establishment and distribution of which the Reverend Gerald B. Winrod had a hand.

get a native American body into the organization so they would have an American "front."

Gilbert opened offices in Washington and, fearful lest their location become known, rented Post Office Box No. 771, Ben Franklin Station, for use as a mailing address. After the first issue had been sent out, Winrod and his agents canvassed prominent industrialists for donations to support the "news service" on the grounds that it was furthering religious activities and fighting Communism. The money collected was actually used to carry on anti-democratic propaganda. A number of industrialists contributed. I have a list of them, but since there is no

The Wessington Springs Independent

C. J. WEBB, PUBLISHER

Wessington Springs, South Dakota

January 19, 1937

Capital News & Feature Service
Ben Franklin Station
Box 771
Washington, D.C.

Gentlemen:-

We are in receipt of a service from you
entitled "Inside News from the Nations Capital,"
by Dan Gilbert, which we do not recollect
ordering. We wish to know the source of this
service, if it is free, and why? We are running
a Washington Service and of course would have to
have some definite reason for changing, and if we
started to use yours we would want the assurance
that it would come regularly, until advance notice
was received to stop it.

Respectfully,

CJW:GB

Letter from a small-town newspaper showing the kind of confusion
caused by the "Capitol News and Feature Service."

conclusive evidence that they knew the money was being spent by Nazi
agents, I shall not publish the names. I mention it merely as an illustration of how wealthy men are victimized by racketeers with pleas of
"patriotism" and "public service." Harry A. Jung did the same thing
by getting money from rich Jews "to fight Communism" and from rich
gentiles "to fight the menace of the Jew."

With the first issue of the *Capitol News and Feature Service,* the following announcement was mailed to the editors of rural weeklies:

"Good Morning, Mr. Editor! *Capitol News and Feature Service* herewith delivers three priceless articles, fresh from the Nation's capitol. Use them without cost. You will hear from us each week. Watch for these interesting articles."

An examination of the "priceless articles" showed that they were designed primarily to attack American democracy.

Since his return from Germany and his conferences at the Nazi Embassy, Winrod has made frequent trips into Mexico where he has met with Mexican fascists—especially with leaders of the Mexican Gold Shirts which were organized by Hermann Schwinn. Again we discover the tie-up between fascist organizations in the United States and those to the south of us.

※　※　※

When the Nazis reorganized their propaganda machine several years ago and established smuggling headquarters on the West Coast, propaganda taken off Nazi ships docking in San Diego and Los Angeles included material printed in Spanish for the special use of General Nicholas Rodriguez, head of the Gold Shirts.

The Spanish as well as the English material was taken to the *Deutsches Haus* in Los Angeles and turned over to Schwinn, who forwarded the batches to Rodriguez. The contact man between Schwinn and the head of the fascist movement in Mexico is a native American named Henry Douglas Allen of San Diego. Allen, under the pretext of being a mining engineer and interested in prospecting in Mexico, went repeatedly into the neighboring country with the smuggled propaganda and delivered it to Rodriguez' agents.

Since native Americans, especially if they say they wish to prospect, can travel across the international boundary into Mexico as often as they please without arousing suspicion, Allen was chosen as the liaison man between Nazi agents in the United States and Rodriguez. As I said earlier, the Nazis tried from the beginning to get an American "front" and to draw as many Americans into it as possible—obviously strategic preparation for future work more serious than mere propaganda. Hence Allen was instructed to become active in the Silver Shirt movement. He organized Down Town Post No. 47-10 and established Silver Shirt recruiting headquarters in Room 693 at 730 South Grand Ave., Los Angeles.

In August, 1936, when a lot of Nazi and anti-Roosevelt money was being shelled out in efforts to defeat Roosevelt, Allen became extremely active. While Pelley was out of town, he was instructed to work with Kenneth Alexander, Pelley's right-hand man. Alexander was formerly a still-photographer at United Artists Studios. The two opened offices in the Broadway Arcade Building and on October 1, 1935, moved to the Lankersheim Building at Third Street near Spring, Los Angeles.

Rodriguez, after he was given assurances of Nazi aid, worked not only with Nazi agents in this country but also with Julio Brunet, manager of the Ford factory in Mexico City.

The earliest documentary record I have of their tie-up is a letter Rodriguez wrote to Ford's manager on September 27, 1934, on Gold Shirt stationery. The letter merely asks Brunet to give jobs to two "worthy young men" and is written in a manner that shows Rodriguez and Brunet are rather close.

By February 7, 1935, Rodriguez and the Ford executive in Mexico had become sufficiently intimate for the fascist leader to express his appreciation of Brunet's placing Gold Shirts in the plant. His letter addressed to the manager of the Ford Company follows:

We have been informed by our delegate, Senora N. M. Colunga, that she was very well treated by you and that in addition you informed her that our request for work for some of our comrades who needed it has also been heard. Not doubting but that this will be fulfilled, A.R.M. [the Gold

Shirts] sends you the most expressive thanks for having seen in you the recognition of one of the greatest obligations of humanity to Mexicanism.

On November 19, 1935, shortly before the Gold Shirts felt they were powerful enough to attempt the overthrow of the Mexican Government and the establishment of a fascist dictatorship, Rodriguez wrote to the manager of the Ford plant, asking for the two ambulances which had been promised the fascists by the Ford manager. Rodriguez had organized his attempted Putsch carefully, with a women's ambulance corps to care for the wounded in the expected fighting. The letter, again translated almost literally, follows:

```
                                    - Se le hace una espe-
                          cial recomendación.

Señor Ing.
JULIO BRUNET.
Gerente de los Talleres "Ford".
Colonia Industrial, D. F.


Muy estimado y fino Ingeniero y amigo:

            Tengo verdadero gusto en presentar a usted por
medio de ésta a los jóvenes don Adolfo y don Gilberto Castañe-
da ambos muy apreciables, hijos de un íntimo amigo mío. Los
jóvenes Castañeda ansiosos de encontrar nuevos horizontes que
les ayuden a solucionar la cotidiana lucha por la vida, han
acudido a mí en demanda de ayuda, y siendo ellos por todos mo-
tivos dignos de lograr su noble aspiración, yo me permito de
la manera más atenta recomendarlos a las finas atenciones de
usted, para que si a bien lo tiene se sirva impartirles su va-
liosa ayuda dándoles oportunidad de que trabajen en esa impor-
tante planta industrial.

            Muy obligado quedaré con usted si se sirve aten-
der la presente súplica por lo que anticipadamente le envío
mis agradecimientos.

            Suyo muy afectuosamente servidor y amigo.


                          Nicolás Rodríguez C.
```

Letter from General Nicholás Rodriguez, Mexican fascist leader, to the Ford manager in Mexico City, soliciting employment for two protégés.

Sr. Manager of the Ford Company   Nov. 19, 1935.
Mexico City

Highly Esteemed Señor:

This will be delivered to you personally by Sr. General Juan Alvarez C., who comes with the object of ascertaining if that company would be able to supply two ambulances which they had already offered, for the transportation of the Women's Sanitary Brigade on the 20th day of this month at 8 a.m.

Thanking you in advance for the references, I am happy to repeat that I am at your command. Affectionately and attentively, S. S.

NICHOLAS RODRIGUEZ C.
Supreme Commander.

In the street fighting that followed the attempted fascist Putsch a number were killed and wounded. It was after this fight that Rodriguez was exiled.

I am reproducing some of these letters from carbon copies, initialed by Rodriguez, which were in his files. Why he initials carbon copies I don't know, but I have a stack of his correspondence with Nazi agents and almost all of his carbons are initialed.

On October 4, 1936, Allen wrote to the exiled fascist leader. Ostensibly the letter invited him to address the Silver Shirts. Actually it was for a special conference about "matters of vital importance to us both." This letter was written when Schwinn was holding conferences with Pelley to merge forces in a fascist united front, and when Schneeberger was preparing to leave for Japan on a training ship ordered up from the Canal Zone by the Japanese to take him on board. The letter follows:

Dear General Rodriguez:

Upon receipt of this letter will you kindly communicate with me and advise me whether it would be possible for you to come to Los Angeles in the near future to make an address to our organization here. We shall be glad to defray all expenses which will include airplane both ways if you desire it. We shall also offer you bodyguard for your protection if you deem it necessary. Your fight is our fight and it is our desire to have you come to Los Angeles especially to confer with us relative to matters of vital importance to us both. I would suggest that if you can arrange to come, you telegraph me (charges collect) upon receipt of this letter so that I may make arrangements without delay.

Fraternally yours,

HENRY ALLEN.

When I went to Mexico to look into Nazi activities, I gave a copy of this letter to the Minister of the Interior. At that time Allen was again in Mexico under the pretense of looking into his mining interests, but a check showed that he had actually gone there to confer secretly with a Mexican army man, General Iturbe. At my request the Mexican Government looked into Allen's movements and learned that he had entered Guaymas, center of Japanese activities, with Kenneth Alexander, Pelley's chief aid.

The connection between Ford's Mexican manager and General Rodriguez might be considered an unfortunate incident for which Ford could not be held responsible. This would be a reasonable assumption if the Nazi-Rodriguez-Ford tie-up in Mexico were an isolated case. The facts, however, show it is not.

```
                              noviembre 19 de 1935.


     Sr. Gerente de la Cia. FORD.
     C i u d a d.


                    Senor de mi respeto:

            La presente le sera entregada personalmente
     por el Sr. General JUAN ALVAREZ C., quien va con el obje-
     to de saber si esa Compania podra facilitar dos ambulan.
     cias que ya con anticipacion habian ofrecido, con objeto.
     del transporte de la Brigada Sanitaria Femenil el dia 20.
     del actual a las 8 a.m.
            Anticipandole las gracias por el favor de refe
     rencia, me es grato repetirme a sus ordenes como su afmo.
     atto., y S.S.




                 ---------------------------
                 NICOLAS RODRIGUEZ C.
                    Jefe Supremo.
```

Letter from General Rodriguez to the Ford manager in
Mexico City. The translation is given on page 112.

The national leader of the Nazi propaganda machine in this country has been on the Ford pay roll. Kuhn was supposed to work for Ford as a chemist, but while on Ford's pay roll he traveled around the United States conferring with other secret Nazi agents and actively directing Nazi work in this country.

Ford has a highly developed and exceedingly efficient espionage system of his own which, among other things, watches what his employees do—even to their home life. Kuhn's activities were known to Harry Bennett, head of the Ford secret service or "Personnel Department," as it is called, and Bennett reports to Ford. Furthermore, Kuhn's Nazi connections had been publicized in both the American and the Nazi press and were no secret. Jews and Christians alike protested to Ford about his employee's anti-democratic work while on the motor magnate's pay roll, but Kuhn was left undisturbed to travel around organizing Nazi groups. In 1938 Ford was given the highest medal of honor which Hitler can give to a foreigner. No statement was ever made as to just what Henry Ford had done for the Nazi Führer to merit the honor.

Simultaneously with Kuhn's intensified work, Ford's confidential secretary, William J. Cameron, became active again. Cameron was

DIVISION HEADQUARTERS

The Silver Battalion

SUITE 713 ARCADE BUILDING
542 SOUTH BROADWAY

LOS ANGELES, CALIFORNIA
October 4, 1936

THE SILVER LEGION OF AMERICA
THE CHRISTIAN PARTY
COUNCILS OF SAFETY
PELLEY'S PUBLISHING

General Nicholas Rodriguez,
El Paso, Texas.

Dear General Roderiguez:

Upon receipt of this letter will you kindly communicate with me and advise me whether it would be possible for you to come to Los Angeles in the near future to make an address to our organization here. We shall be glad to defray all expenses which will include aero-plan both ways if you desire it. We shall also offer you body guard for your protection if you deem it necessary. Your fight is our fight and it is our desire to have you come to Los Angeles especially to confer with us relative to matters of vital importance to us both. I would suggest that if you can arrange to come, that you telegraph me (charges collect) upon receipt of this letter so that I may make arrangements without delay.

Fraternally yours,

A/p

Henry Allen.

Letter from Henry Allen to General Rodriguez, showing the tie-up between American and Mexican fascist organizations.

LEFT: *American-made anti-Semitic sticker of a type appearing with increasing frequency in recent times.* RIGHT: *Title-page of the German edition of "The International Jew," by Henry Ford, of which 100,000 copies have been distributed.*

editor of Ford's *Dearborn Independent* when that newspaper published the "Protocols of the Elders of Zion" after they had been proved to be forgeries. When a nation-wide protest arose from Jews and Christians who were shocked at seeing one of the richest and most powerful men in the country use his wealth to disseminate race hatred, and when the protest grew into a boycott of his cars, Ford apologized and discontinued the newspaper. But instead of easing his editor out or giving him some other job, he made him his confidential secretary.

When Kuhn went to work for Ford, the national headquarters of the Nazi propaganda machine was moved to Detroit, and the anti-democratic activities increased in intensity. Employing Nazi antisemitism as the bait to attract dissatisfied and bewildered elements in the population, a new organization made its appearance: The Anglo-Saxon Federation, headed by Ford's private secretary. Headquarters were established in the McCormick Building in Chicago, Room 834, at 332 S. Michigan Ave. and in the Fox Building in Detroit.

In July, 1936, Cameron, obviously because Ford was violently anti-Roosevelt, stepped out as head of the organization and became its Director of Publications. When Winrod was raising money from American industrialists to support the *Capitol News and Feature Service,* Cameron was among the contributors.

The Anglo-Saxon Federation began to distribute the "Protocols" again. I bought a copy in the Detroit offices of the organization, stamped with the name of the organization. The introduction quotes Ford as approving of them. It states:

Mr. Henry Ford, in an interview published in the *New York World,* February 17, 1921, put the case for Nilus[17] tersely and convincingly thus:

"The only statement I care to make about the 'Protocols' is that they fit in with what is going on. They are sixteen years old, and they have fitted the world situation up to this time. They fit it now."

When Ford was on the witness stand in a libel suit some fifteen years ago and admitted his ignorance of matters with which even grammar school children are familiar, the country laughed. His ignorance, however, is his own affair, but when he takes no step to curb his personal representative from working with secret foreign agents to undermine a friendly government, it becomes a matter, it appears to me, of importance to the people of this country and the Government of the United States.

17 The man who forged the "Protocols" originally and who subsequently confessed to having done so.

IX NAZI AGENTS IN AMERICAN UNIVERSITIES

THE UNIVERSITIES ARE TOO IMPORTANT A TRAINING GROUND for Nazi agents to ignore. A few professors in some of our universities have joined the growing list of anti-democratic propagandists. Some of them are German subjects and do not disguise their pro-Nazi bias; others carry on their propaganda as a "scholarly analysis" of the Hitler regime—with a fervor, however, that smacks of the paid propagandist.

German exchange students, too, studying at some of our universities, are active in various efforts to draw native Americans within the sphere of Nazi influence. Some of these students came here ostensibly to study for degrees, but devote most of their time to spreading Nazi ideology and meeting with secret Nazi agents and military spies. Such was Prince von Lippe of the University of Southern California.

Von Lippe is not an American citizen as so many of the agents are. With no visible means of support, he received expenses from a total stranger—oddly enough, Count von Bülow whose home overlooked the naval base in San Diego and who was constantly in conferences with Nazi agents. It was to Count von Bülow, you recall, that Hermann Schwinn brought Schneeberger as soon as he arrived on his way to Japan, and von Bülow took him around while Schneeberger photographed areas in the military and naval zone. A number of very secret conferences were held while Schneeberger was on the West Coast, in the home of Dr. K. Burchardi, a Los Angeles physician who visits Nazi ships with Schwinn and von Bülow (on one occasion Schneeberger summoned Burchardi to come with him to a Nazi ship which had just docked in Los Angeles—and the physician dropped his work and went).

German exchange students, when they enter this country, are under instructions to report to the German-American Bund. On July 4, 1936, three exchange students—a young lady and two young men—entered Los Angeles while on a motor tour of the country. They were students at Georgia Tech. In Los Angeles they went directly to the *Deutsches Haus* and presented a letter of introduction to Hermann Schwinn who assigned them quarters at the home of Max Edgan, one of Schwinn's lieutenants. The students then made a detailed report to Schwinn on the political work they were carrying out at Georgia Tech.

But the professors are the chief hope of Nazi agents attempting to spread the idea of totalitarian government and a bit of race hatred as the bait to attract some elements in the population. Some of the professors and some of their activities follow briefly:

▪ ▫ ▨

Professor Frederick E. Auhagen, formerly of the German Department, Seth Low Junior College, Columbia University.

Dr. Auhagen came to this country in 1923 and worked as a mining engineer in Pennsylvania. From 1925 to 1927 he was with the Foreign Department of the Equitable Trust Co.; then became connected with Columbia University in 1927. He is not an American citizen and constantly refers to Germany as "my native country."

This professor is one of the leading academic apologists for Herr Hitler in the United States. Besides carrying on his pro-Nazi propaganda in the classroom, he does a great deal of lecturing, sometimes appearing before the Foreign Policy Association. On one occasion, in an address before the Men's Club of the Baptist Church at Rockville, Long Island, he stated that Seth Low Junior College was opened "in order to keep Hebrew faces off the campus at Columbia University."

Auhagen never tried to hide his sympathies with Nazism. Preceding a debate on February 1, 1936, before the City Club of Cleveland, he gave press interviews as a Nazi, and in the debate upheld Hitler as the savior of Germany and world civilization. With a fervor far removed from professorial calm, he explained that American newspaper dispatches about the treatment of Jews and Catholics in Germany were exaggerated.

"As to criticism of Germany's treatment of Catholics," he said again in Denver, Colorado on July 26, 1935, "that is not true!"

※ ※ ※

Professor Frederick K. Krueger, of Wittenberg college, with whom Auhagen is rather closely identified in arranging and giving talks about Nazis and totalitarian government, at every opportunity issues press interviews along the same line. In them he explains that the anti-Nazi sentiment in the United States press does not represent the editors, but is dictated by Jews who "control the press, the motion pictures and other organs of public opinion."

※ ※ ※

Because of the high scientific standing of Professor Vladimir Karapetoff of the Cornell engineering faculty, he is listened to with more attention and respect than are the more blatant propagandists for the adoption of fascist tactics and principles. Shortly after Hitler took power, the Professor started to do his share on the campus. At first he did it subtly, but when this made little headway he began to talk of the "growing domination of Jews in American life, politically as well as economically" and emphasized that the large number of Jews in the Law School and on the campus generally was becoming a problem.

"It's the smooth-faced Jew whom we must fear," he kept repeating, "and not the long-bearded Jewish rabbi."

Not content with expressing personal opinions, he took to organizing groups, addressing them on the subject of the Jew; and on one occasion he called a special meeting of the Officer's Club with the proviso that Jews be excluded.

※ ※ ※

Paul F. Douglas,[18] teacher of German, Economics and Political Science at Green Mountain College, wrote a book, *God Among the Germans,* which purports to be an introduction to the mind and method of Nazism.

I have information coming from a reputable source that Dr. Douglas was paid by the Nazi Government to write the book. This source is unwilling to let his name be used, but is ready to testify and lay his information before any governmental body which will investigate the devious methods of Nazi agents in this country.

※ ※ ※

There are at various universities throughout the country other professors and instructors quite active in spreading pro-Hitler propaganda. Some of them meet with Nazi agents closely allied to the espionage machine. I offer only these few as illustrations of Nazi efforts to get footholds in the American universities.

---

18 Not to be confused with Prof. Paul H. Douglas of the University of Chicago, a highly reputable scholar and a stanch defender of democracy.

Along with efforts to carry on their work in the universities, Nazi agents tried to get a foothold in the political life of the country by finding a few Republicans who were willing to use anti-democratic propaganda in their efforts to defeat Roosevelt during the Presidential campaign. At no time in American history did secret agents of a foreign power so brazenly attempt to interfere in the internal affairs of the American people. Nor at any time in American history did agents of a foreign government find such willing cooperation from unscrupulous American politicians.

Among those who worked with Hitler agents was Newton Jenkins, director of the Coughlin-Lemke Third Party.[19] The Detroit Priest and the Congressman were fully aware, preceding and during the campaign, that Jenkins supported Hitler and was a Jew-baiter of the first order. They were aware of this while they were appealing for Jewish votes. The Radio Priest and the Congressman kept in constant touch with their campaign manager and knew what sort of government Jenkins wanted.

Jenkins' association with Nazis dates to the days preceding the launching of the Presidential campaign. At that time he participated in a secret conference held in Chicago with the object of uniting the scattered fascist forces in the United States to form a powerful fascist united front. Among those who attended where Walter Kappe, Fritz Gissibl and Zahn—three active Hitler agents assigned to the Mid-West area; William Dudley Pelley, leader of the Silver Shirts; Harry A. Jung, the ultra-"patriot"; George W. Christians of Chattanooga, Tenn., head of the American fascists; and several others. The conference ended with an agreement to support a Third-Party movement directed by Jenkins.

---

19 Father Coughlin was finally reprimanded by the Vatican for his unpriestly attacks upon the President.

Throughout the campaign Jenkins stressed an exaggerated nationalism, advocated "party patrols" similar to Hitler's storm troops and adopted the Nazi Jew-baiting tactics. His first public appearance with the Nazis was on October 30, 1935, at a meeting held in Lincoln Turner Hall, 1005 Diversey Building, Chicago. Uniformed storm troopers with the swastika on their arm bands patrolled the room. In the course of his talk he said:

> The trouble with this country now is due to the money powers and Jewish politicians who control our Government. The Federal Treasury is being controlled by a Jew, Morgenthau, and a Jew, Eugene Meyer. The State, County and our own Municipal Government is being controlled by Jewish politicians. Our own Mayor signs what the Jews want him to sign. Nearly in every department of our country and local government you will find a Jew at the head of it. Not only under a Democratic administration but also under a Republican administration we will find the same conditions. . . . The American people must free itself from the money plunderers who have thrown this country into the World War and also a possibility of dragging them into the present war for private gain and shake off their shoulders the Jewish politicians. The Third Party promises to do both.

This is precisely the sort of stuff paid Nazi agents in the propaganda division are ordered to disseminate, and this is the man Father Coughlin and Congressman Lemke picked to direct their campaign.

▥   ▤   ▥

It was a Nazi agent, Ernst Goerner of Milwaukee, who spread the story, aided by anti-Roosevelt forces, that Frances Perkins, Secretary of Labor, was a Jewess. The story received such wide publicity that she had to issue a public statement giving her birth and marriage records.

Goerner is one of the important Nazi agents in the Mid-West. He's a bit eccentric and the Nazis sometimes have difficulty keeping him in line, but when Schwinn made a trip East shortly before the election campaign, he stopped off specially to see Goerner who thereupon sent a flood of propaganda throughout the country about Secretary Perkins' ancestry as well as charges that Roosevelt and almost all Government officials were Jews.

It was after Schwinn's trip to the East that other disseminators of anti-democratic propaganda, like Robert Edward Edmondson and James True, came to life in a big way. One of the penniless men who suddenly blossomed into the money after Schwinn's trip East was Olov E. Tietzow, who used Post Office Box No. 491 in Chicago lest the fact that he lived at 715 Aldine Ave. be discovered.

Up until a few months before the campaign Tietzow was an unemployed electrical engineer who had difficulty paying the three-dollar weekly rent for his hall bed-room at the Aldine Ave. address. After Schwinn's visit and meeting with him, Tietzow began to commute by air between Chicago and Buffalo where he opened a branch office.

Tietzow was tested out a little at first. He was put to work in the offices of the Friends of the New Germany on Western Ave. and Roscoe St., Chicago. In his spare time he worked out of 1454 Foster Ave., Chicago. A quotation or two from some of his letters will give an indication of his activities. On February 21, 1936, he wrote to William Stern, Fargo, N. D., a member of the Republican National Committee. He said in part:

> Information about the so-called fascist movement here in the U.S. A. will be furnished by me if you so desire, together with other data you might be interested in. An opportunity to discuss

our national problems and to lay before patriotic persons of means and influence and before national organizations my plans for a nationwide movement would be welcome. . . .

This letter to a high Republican Party official was written after Tietzow had outlined the contents to Toni Mueller, Nazi agent in Chicago reporting directly to Fritz Kuhn.

Since most of the patrioteers were opposed to the New Deal and since some of them were already working with Nazi agents in this country, it was not long before they were going full blast in their "Save America" racket. The people of the United States, though they don't talk much about it, are thoroughly patriotic in the fullest sense of the word. To accuse anyone of not being a patriot is almost worse than telling a man that he is a son of not quite a lady. The racketeers in patriotism long ago discovered that people would contribute to a "patriotic cause" if only to escape the reputation of being unpatriotic; and the racketeers have made a nice living out of it. For some of the patrioteers it has become a thriving business, with everybody involved—except the suckers—getting his cut. Some of the big "patriotic" organizations are really influential, and the small ones are hopefully struggling along in the expectation of bigger and better and more patriotic days when the pickings will be more than attractive.

Every time I start looking into organizations with high-sounding and impressive names, I am profoundly impressed with the accuracy of Barnum's noted observation. Raise the cry of "patriotism" and perfectly good Americans forget to try to find out just what the "patriotic" activities are, and shell out without a murmur. Industrialists particularly like the "Americanism" of the patriotic groups because almost all of them incorporate an anti-labor policy. The propaganda, of course, is

©1936 - O.E.T.

THE AMERICAN GUARD

8-15-1936

Mr. Warner W. Pearson, Architect,
6 North Michigan Ave.,
Chicago, Illinois.

Dear Mr. Pearson:

Received your request for literature. From time to time, pamphlets dealing with the Jewish-Communistic problems will be sent to you. Extra copies of especially interesting ones will be sent to you with request that you distribute them among your friends; there is no charge for any of those leaflets.

The American Guard is now being organized by me in the states of Illinois and Minnesota, and later on the activities will be extended to other states as well. The purpose is to help counteract the undermining influence of Jews and other communists, and to restore White rule here in America. Members of the organization do not, for the time being, pay any fees or dues; reliance is made entirely upon voluntary contributions. — The main activities now center upon distribution of educational propaganda; active participation in politics will start in a couple of months when, I hope, the organization of this party has been completed.

Trusting that you will actively support the organization, I am

Sincerely yours,
Olov E. Tietzow
P.O.Box 491, Chicago, Illinois

Letter by Olov E. Tietzow, showing typical methods of American fascists.

rarely conducted as an open fight against labor, but is put across as a fight to save America from the Communists.

Some of the racketeering patriotic organizations with a more or less devout following include the National Republican Publishing Company, Washington, D. C., the American Vigilant Intelligence Federation, Chicago, Ill., the Paul Reveres, Chicago, Ill., the Industrial Defense Association, Boston, Mass., the American Nationalists, Inc., New York, N.Y. and the American Nationalist Party, Los Angeles, Calif. There are a number of others, but these are some of the most blatant.

⸻ ⸻ ⸻

The National Republican Company, 511 11th Street, N.W., Washington, D.C., is one of the most influential. It publishes the *National Republic,* a journal accepted by men high in public office and by leading industrialists as earnestly trying to inculcate "Americanism" into Americans.

The *National Republic* has an amazing list of endorsers—governors, mayors, senators, congressmen and nationally-known industrialists. The magazine is virtually the entire organization and is dedicated "to defending American ideals and institutions." It is headed by Walter S. Steele, who was tied up with Harry A. Jung of the American Vigilant Intelligence Federation before he went into business for himself. While Steele was working with the ace of racketeers in patriotism, the president-editor of the *National Republic* also eked out a few pennies by distributing the "Protocols of the Elders of Zion." Today, however, he confines himself chiefly to fighting Communism, spreading race hatred only when it is paid for in advertisements. Books distributed by Nazi propagandists in furthering their anti-democratic campaign—such books as *T.N.T.* by Colonel Edwin Hadley and *The Conflict of the Ages* find space in the *National Republic's* pages. Colonel Hadley headed the

Paul Reveres which tried to organize fascist groups on American university campuses, and *The Conflict of the Ages* devotes a full chapter to the Nazi "proofs" of the authenticity of the "Protocols."

I mention these to show the type of stuff Steele is willing to disseminate—if he is paid for it. And by permitting the use of their names, the sponsors, consciously or unconsciously, aid him in his anti-American activities.

The detailed aims of the *National Republic* are to provide a "weekly service to twenty-three hundred editors, to defend American institutions against subversive radicalism; a national information service on subversive organizations and activities; an Americanization bureau serving schools, colleges and patriotic groups; conducted for the public good from Washington, D.C., by nationally known leaders."

The procedure of conducting the organization "for the public good" includes high-pressuring the shekels from the suckers. Steele, a former newspaperman, learned from his association with that other arch-patriot, Jung. So when Steele established his own racket, he found one of his early aids in former Senator Robinson of Indiana. Robinson was closely tied up with the Ku Klux Klan. Through Robinson and through other politicians reached with the cry "Save America," he got a long list of prominent sponsors and gradually increased it until now it reads like a *Who's Who* of reactionary industrialists and innocent politicians. With letters of introduction from Senator Robinson, Steele's high pressure gang set out to collect in the name of patriotism.

The procedure was simple. Salesmen presented their letters of introduction to the mayor of a city. The mayor was impressed with the high "patriotic" motives and especially with the imposing list of names sponsoring the efforts. The mayor introduced the high-pressure fellows to other people—and the milking began.

Let me illustrate a little more specifically:

On March 4, 1936, Steele sent two of his ablest dollar-pullers, Messrs. Fahr and Hamilton, into the Oklahoma oil fields where the industrialists would like to see a minimum of 200 per cent Americanism instilled in the public mind. Messrs. Fahr and Hamilton had letters of introduction to Mayor T. A. Penny of Tulsa, Okla. When the salesmen approached the Mayor, they had not only the long and imposing list of names on the letterhead but additional letters of introduction from ex-Governor Curley of Mass., ex-Senator Robinson of Indiana and Congressman Martin Dies of Texas. The drummers wanted the Mayor to introduce them to the Chairman of the Tulsa Board of Education who could help them get funds in Tulsa and elsewhere. The funds were to be used to place the "patriotic" magazine in the public school system in order "to preserve this country against subversive activities, particularly Communism."

It was a neat circulation-getting stunt, performed without Fahr and Hamilton telling what percentage of the take they got.

The Mayor gave the letters of introduction. With these letters and the excellent contacts thus established, they started down the sucker list from W. G. Skelly, head of the Skelly Oil Co., Tulsa to Waite Phillips of the Phillips Petroleum Co.

Like his former colleague Harry A. Jung, Steele works on the big industrialists by whispering confidentially that he has sources of information about which he can't talk much but which make it possible for him to keep the industrialists informed about "subversive radicals." For a reasonable price and perhaps a contribution to a worthy cause, Steele would supply the industrialist with "confidential information for members only" which would keep him up to date about the radicals threatening America. The "confidential information" must not be shown to anybody else. Extreme caution is necessary lest the radicals find out about the "information service." With all this hocum, secrecy and whispering, the industrialist becomes a member at so much per not realizing that the information thus peddled can be got for three cents a day—five cents on Sundays—by buying the *Daily Worker*. It's just one of the little patriotic rackets the boys have cooked up.

Working closely with Steele is James A. True of the James True Associates, another precious racketeer who stepped from patrioteering into efforts to organize in conjunction with Nazi agents a secret armed force in the United States. With True in this effort to establish a Cagoulard organization in this country, were some of the most active Nazi agents and patrioteers.

X UNDERGROUND ARMIES IN AMERICA

EARLY IN 1938 NATIVE AMERICANS, working with Nazi agents, completed plans to organize a secret army along the general lines of the Cagoulards in France. The decision was made after the liaison man between Nazi agents here and plotters for the secret army met with Fritz Kuhn and Signor Giuseppe Cosmelli, Counselor to the Italian Embassy in Washington.

The liaison man is Henry D. Allen, who moved from San Diego to 2860 Nina St., Pasadena, Calif. Allen, the reader may recollect, helped Schwinn organize the Mexican Gold Shirts which unsuccessfully attempted to seize the Mexican Government. Allen is still active in a plot to overthrow the Cárdenas Government, working at the moment with Gen. Ramon F. Iturbe, a member of the Mexican Chamber of Deputies, with Gen. Yocupicio who is smuggling arms as part of a plan to rebel, and with Pablo L. Delgado who took over the fascist Gold Shirt work under a different name after Rodriguez was exiled when his attempt to march on the Government failed.

To understand the feverish activities of foreign agents and native Americans working with foreign agents, one must remember that when the World War broke out in 1914, Germany was caught with only small espionage and sabotage organizations in the United States. It cost the German War Office large sums of money to build them under difficult and dangerous conditions. The Nazis do not intend to be caught the same way in the event a war finds the United States on the enemy side or, if neutral, supplying arms and materials to the enemy.

The first step to prevent such a development is to build an enormous propaganda machine and to draw into it as many native Americans as possible. Because of the future potentialities of natives as spies and *saboteurs,* the Nazi leaders take extraordinary precautions to safeguard their identities. Should the United States become involved in a war with fascist powers, especially Germany, the German members of the Bund can be watched and, if necessary, interned; but native Americans not known as Bund members can move about freely, hence the care to prevent their identities from becoming known. Schwinn, for instance, keeps a regular list of the German-American Bund members at the *Deutsches Haus* in Los Angeles. The native American members, however, are not listed. The names are kept in code and only Schwinn knows the code numbers.

Military considerations thus lead the Nazi General Staff to maintain this propaganda in the United States, despite the knowledge Nazi leaders in Germany have that its activities and distasteful propaganda here are seriously hampering German-American commercial relations.

The propaganda machine is already functioning as the German-American *Volksbund.* The second step, as was demonstrated in France with the Cagoulards and in Spain with Franco's Fifth Column, is to organize secret armies capable of starting sporadic outbreaks tantamount to civil war—a procedure which would naturally deflect the country's energies in war time.

This second step was taken after careful study, and Henry D. Allen was chosen as the liaison man between those maneuvering the plot.

The private letters exchanged between Allen and his fellow conspirators are now in my possession. Some of the letters exchanged were signed with the writers' real names and some with code names. Allen's code name, for instance, is "Rosenthal."

On April 13, 1938, he wrote to a "G.D." (of whom more shortly) as follows:

Have just sent Delgado into Sonora incognito. This move has resulted from a four-party conference held in Yuma a few days ago. This party was composed of Urbalejo, chief of the Yaqui nation, Joe Mattus, his trusted lieutenant, Delgado and myself. Yocupicio has completely come over to our side, which you can perceive from the outcome of the little tryout in Aqua Prieta a few weeks ago. Delgado has arrived safely at Bocatete, and will get the boys in that part of the country pretty active. . . . Inasmuch as I am his legal and properly accredited representative in the United States, you may rest assured that there will be no doubt as to the objectives of this movement south of the Rio Grande.

I have received three letters from General Iturbe in which he tells me that they are taking the Spanish copies of the Protocols which K. sent me, and making 5,000 copies of same. In each letter he begs me to set a time and date for meeting him at Guadalajara for the purpose of effecting the necessary plans for active campaigning with Delgado. I will arrange all of this as soon as you consider it expedient. . . .

ROSENTHAL.

Two days later (April 15, 1938) he wrote from Fresno, Calif. under his own name to F. W. Clark, 919½ S. Yakima Ave., Tacoma, Wash. The letter reads in part:

Relative to the Gold Shirts of Mexico, please be advised that we found it necessary to reorganize this group in August, 1937. The activist elements have proceeded and are now carrying on under the name of the Mexican Nationalist Movement of which Pablo L. Delgado is the nominal head. I am the legal and personal representative of Delgado in the movement in the United States.

So much for his current activities to establish fascism to the south of us.

Most Americans who fall for Nazi propaganda do not suspect that they are being played for suckers by shrewd manipulators pulling the strings in Berlin, and probably not one of the many reputable and sincerely patriotic Americans who fell for Allen's "patriotic" appeals suspects his activities against the country he so zealously wants to "save."

Some shrewd observer once remarked that "patriotism is the last refuge of a scoundrel." Whenever I come across an "ultra-patriot" with foam dripping from his mouth while he beats his chest with loud cries about his own honesty and the crookedness of those running the country, I suspect a phony. As a rule, I look for the criminal record of a man who's yelling "Chase out the crooks" and "Let's have honest government," and all too often I find one. Henry D. Allen, *alias* H. O. Moffet, *alias* Howard Leighton Allen, *alias* Rosenthal, etc., ex-inmate of San Quentin and Folsom prisons, is no exception; his criminal record extends over a period of twenty-nine years.

Let me give the record before I start quoting from his letters, chiefly for the benefit of those sincere and loyal Americans who thought his Swastika-inspired activities represented honest convictions.

May 17, 1910: Arrested in Los Angeles charged with uttering fictitious checks. In simple language this means just a little bit of forgery. Los Angeles Police Department file, No. 7613.

June 10, 1910: Sentenced to three years imprisonment; sentence suspended upon tearful assurances of good behavior.

May 12, 1912: Picked up in Philadelphia charged with being a fugitive; brought back to Los Angeles.

July 1, 1912: Committed to San Quentin. Guest No. 25835.

April 21, 1915: Committed to Folsom from Santa Barbara on a forgery charge. Guest No. 9542.

Feb. 1, 1919: Arrested in Los Angeles County charged with suspicion of a felony. Los Angeles County No. 14554.

June 31, 1924: Arrested in San Francisco, charged with uttering fictitious checks. No. 35570.

Oct. 5, 1925: Los Angeles Police Department issued notice that Allen was wanted for uttering fictitious checks. Bulletin No. 233.

Allen is apparently a prolific writer—of bad checks and of long reports about his activities to his superiors.

Two of Allen's close friends are also native Americans: C. F. Ingalls of 2702 Bush St., San Francisco and George Deatherage (the G. D. mentioned earlier). Deatherage now lives and operates out of St. Albans, W. Va. He organized the American Nationalist Confederation which used to have its headquarters in Palo Alto, Calif. Both these gentlemen also work with Schwinn.

On January 7, 1938, Deatherage received from San Francisco a letter signed "C.F.I."—in a plain envelope without a return address. The letter is very long and detailed. I quote in part:

> We must get busy organizing grid-lattice-work or skeleton for a military staff throughout the nation, and in this we need representatives of fascist groups, and we need Americans with whom these others may be incorporated. . . . All must believe in being ruthless in an emergency. . . .
>
> The political and the military organizations must not be unified. They have different aims. With one hand we offer the public a potential program. Whether they accept it or not and whether they wish to return to the ideals embodied in a representative form of a constitutional federal republic or not, is of secondary importance. Of first importance is the need of the emergency military organization to function simultaneously should our enemies revolt if we should win politically or should we revolt if our enemies win politically.

On January 19, 1938, Deatherage received a letter signed with the code name "Laura and Clayton." "Laura" is Hermann Schwinn. This letter, too, is long and goes into details on how best to organize the secret military group and have it ready for instant action. The letter states at one point:

> After we do all this, now then we shall have the national military frame-work all steamed up and oiled and coupled to the multiplicity of working parts ready to appear on all fronts. . . .

After "C.F.I." and "Laura and Clayton" had decided on the details of the secret military body in which they needed the aid of "Nazi and fascist" forces, they needed money and arms.

Early in January, Allen received from "Mrs. Fry and C. Chapman" four hundred and fifty dollars for a trip to Washington, D. C. "Mrs. Fry and C. Chapman" live in Santa Monica, but use Glendale, Calif. for a post office address. This money was spent between January 13 and February 10, 1938, according to the expense account Allen turned in to the Fry-Chapman combination.

Three days after Allen got the money (January 16, 1938), he received from Schwinn a letter of introduction to Fritz Kuhn, addressed to the *Amerikadeutscher Volksbund,* 178 E. 85th Street, New York City. The letter was written in German. Following is the translation:

My Bund Leader:

The bearer of this letter is my old friend and comrade-in-arms, Henry Allen, who is coming East on an important matter.

Mr. Allen knows the situation in Los Angeles and California very well and can give you important information. We can give Allen absolute confidence.

Hail and Victory,

HERMANN SCHWINN.

The "important matter" on which Allen was going East and which he wanted to discuss with the national Nazi leader in this country, was to contact the Italian Embassy, the Hungarian Legation, James True of the James True Associates (distributors of "Industrial Control Reports" from its headquarters in Washington, D.C.), George Deatherage in St. Albans, W. Va., and several others.

Allen reported regularly to Chapman, signing his letters with the code name "Rosenthal." I quote in part from one letter written from Washington on January 24, 1938:

> Upon calling at the Rumanian Embassy I found the Ambassador with all his attachés are of the Carol-Tartarescu regime, and they are sailing on Wednesday, January 26. The new Ambassador will arrive with his staff on Saturday, I am told. The letter which you gave me I mailed to Budapest myself, not daring to entrust it to the present staff at the Embassy. At the Italian Embassy I found the Ambassador away, but I had a very delightful and satisfactory conference with Signor G. Cosmelli, who is the Italian counselor. . . .

Shortly after the conference at the Italian Embassy, True and Allen conferred. Subsequently, True wrote to Allen and added a postscript in long hand: "But be very careful about controlling the information and destroy this letter."

Allen did not destroy it immediately. The letter, dated February 23, 1938, reads in part:

> The bunch of money promised off and on for three years may come through within the next week or two. We have had so many disappointments that I hardly dare hope but there seems a fair chance of results. If it comes through we will have you back here in a hurry. You, George, and I will get together and prepare for real action.
>
> If your friends want some pea shooters, I have connections now for any quantity and at the right price. They are United States standard surplus. Let me know as soon as you can.

To these events must be added the peculiar and unexplained actions of the Dies Congressional Committee appointed to "investigate subversive activities." The Committee employed a Nazi propagandist as one of its chief investigators and refused to question three suspected Nazi spies working in the Brooklyn Navy Yard. Congressman Martin Dies of Texas, chairman of the Committee, gave two of the *National Republic's* high-pressure men letters of introduction when they started out on a little milking party in the name of patriotism. He received the cooperation of Harry A. Jung, and he refused to examine the files of James A. True when the above letter was brought to his Committee's attention.

But these actions merit more detailed consideration.

XI THE DIES COMMITTEE SUPPRESSES EVIDENCE

THREE SUSPECTED NAZI SPIES WERE quietly taken out of the Brooklyn Navy Yard to the Dies Congressional Committee headquarters in New York in Room 1604, United States Court House Building. The three men were each questioned for about five minutes by Congressman J. Parnell Thomas[20] of New Jersey and Joe Starnes of Alabama. The men were asked if they had heard of any un-American goings-on in the Navy Yard. Each of the three subpoenaed men said he had not, and the Congressmen sent them back to work in the Navy Yard after warning them not to say a word to anyone about having been called before the Committee.

When I learned of the Congressional Committee's refusal to question men they had subpoenaed, I wondered at the unusual procedure—especially since it promptly put Nazi propagandists (such as Edwin P. Banta, a speaker for the German-American Bund) on the stand as authorities on "un-American" activities in the United States. A little inquiry turned up some interesting facts.

20 Formerly known as J. Parnell Feeney. He changed his name because he thought he could get along better in the business world with a name like Thomas than with a name as potently Irish as Feeney.

One of the Committee's chief investigators, Edward Francis Sullivan of Boston, had worked closely with Nazi agents as far back as 1934. Sullivan's whole record was extremely unsavory. He had been a labor spy, had been active in promoting anti-democratic sentiments in cooperation with secret agents of the German Government and in addition was a convicted thief. (Shortly after Slap-Happy Eddie, as he was known around Boston because of his convictions on drunkenness, lined up with the Nazis, he got six months for a little stealing.) Before going on with the Congressional Committee's strange attitude toward suspected spies and known propagandists in constant communication with Germany, it might be well to review a meeting which the Congressional Committee's investigator addressed in the Nazi stronghold in Yorkville.

On the night of Tuesday, June 5, 1934, at eight o'clock, some 2,500 Nazis and their friends attended a mass meeting of the Friends of the New Germany at Turnhall, Lexington Ave. and 85th Street, New York City. Sixty Nazi Storm Troopers—attired in uniforms with black breeches and Sam Brown belts, smuggled off Nazi ships—were the guard of honor. Storm Troop officers had white and red arm bands with the swastika superimposed on them. Every twenty minutes the Troopers, clicking their heels in the best Nazi fashion, changed guard in front of the speakers' stand. The Hitler Youth organization was present. Men and women Nazis sold the official Nazi publication, *Jung Sturm,* and everybody awaited the coming of one of the chief speakers of the evening who was to bring them a message from the Boston Nazis.

W. L. McLaughlin, then editor of the *Deutsche Zeitung,* spoke in English. He was followed by H. Hempel, an officer of the Nazi steamship "Stuttgart," who vigorously exhorted his audience to fight for Hitlerism and was rewarded by shouts of "Heil Hitler!" McLaughlin then introduced Edward Francis Sullivan of Boston as a "fighting Irishman."

The gentleman whom the Congressional Committee chose as one of its investigators into subversive activities, gave the crowd the Hitler salute and launched into an attack upon the "dirty, lousy, stinking Jews." In the course of his talk he announced proudly that he had organized the group of Nazis in Boston who had attacked and beaten liberals and Communists at a meeting protesting the docking of the Nazi cruiser "Karlsruhe," in an American port.

The audience cheered. Sullivan, again giving the Nazi salute, shouted: "Throw the goddam lousy Jews—all of them—into the Atlantic Ocean. We'll get rid of the stinking kikes! Heil Hitler!"

The three suspected Nazi spies were subpoenaed on August 23, 1938. They were:

Walter Dieckhoff, Badge No. 38117, living at 2654 E. 19th Street, Sheepshead Bay.

Hugo Woulters, Badge No. 38166, living at 221 East 16th Street, Brooklyn.

Alfred Boldt, Badge No. 38069, living at 64-29 70th Street, Middle Village, L. I.

Boldt had worked in the Navy Yard since 1931. Dieckhoff and Woulters went to work there within one day of each other in June, 1936.

The three men were kept in the Committee's room from one o'clock on the day they were subpoenaed until five in the afternoon. When it became apparent that the Congressmen would not show up until the next day, the men were dismissed and told to come back the following morning.

Not a word was said to them as to why they had been subpoenaed. Nevertheless Dieckhoff, who was with the German Air Corps during the

The Commonwealth of Massachusetts

MIDDLESEX, ss.   AT THE FIRST DISTRICT COURT OF EASTERN MIDDLESEX,
holden at Malden, in the County of Middlesex, for the
transaction of criminal business, on the   fourth
day of   February   in the year of our Lord
one thousand nine hundred and ~~twenty~~   thirty-two

Edward Francis Sullivan , defendant,
is brought before said Court, in due ~~form of law, to answer to~~ THE COMMONWEALTH
OF MASSACHUSETTS, on a complaint, duly made under oath, a true copy of which is
herewith transmitted.

Which complaint is read to the said defendant, and   he is
asked by the Court whether   he is guilty or not guilty of the offence charged against him
in said complaint, and said defendant pleads and says that   he   is ~~not~~
guilty, ~~and the further consideration of said complaint is then, of from time to time,~~
~~continued to the   day of~~
~~then next ensuing,~~ and after hearing the witnesses in the case duly sworn, and fully hearing
and understanding the defence of said defendant, it appears to said Court that said
defendant is guilty of the offence aforesaid.

IT IS THEREFORE CONSIDERED AND ORDERED BY THE COURT,
that the said defendant, for the offence aforesaid,
~~pay a fine of   dollars, or the sum prescribed by law, and~~
~~that he stand committed until said sentence be complied with~~
                                             Billerica
be committed to the House of Correction, in ~~Cambridge~~,

there to be kept ~~and~~ governed according to law ~~and the~~ rules and regulations thereof, for
the term of   six   ~~days~~ —months,—from said last mentioned day.
And ~~the said defendant is~~ thereupon notified by said Court of
his   right to appeal from said conviction and sentence.
ATTEST:— *Wilfred O. Tyler*
                                             Clerk.

From which sentence the said defendant appeals to the SUPERIOR COURT, next to be
holden at Cambridge, within and for the County of Middlesex, for the transaction of criminal
business, on the first Monday of   March   next, and   he is ordered
~~to be held on his   own recognizance,~~ recognize to the Commonwealth,—in the
sum of   Two thousand   ~~hundred~~ dollars,—with sufficient
surety,—to prosecute said appeal there as the law directs—and stand committed to abide
the sentence of said Court thereon, until   he so recognizes.
With which said order the said defendant refuses to comply and is
committed.
ATTEST: *Wilfred O. Tyler* Clerk.

A true copy, Attest:
                    Wilfred B. Tyler, Clerk.
(L. S.)

4-20-31-1000

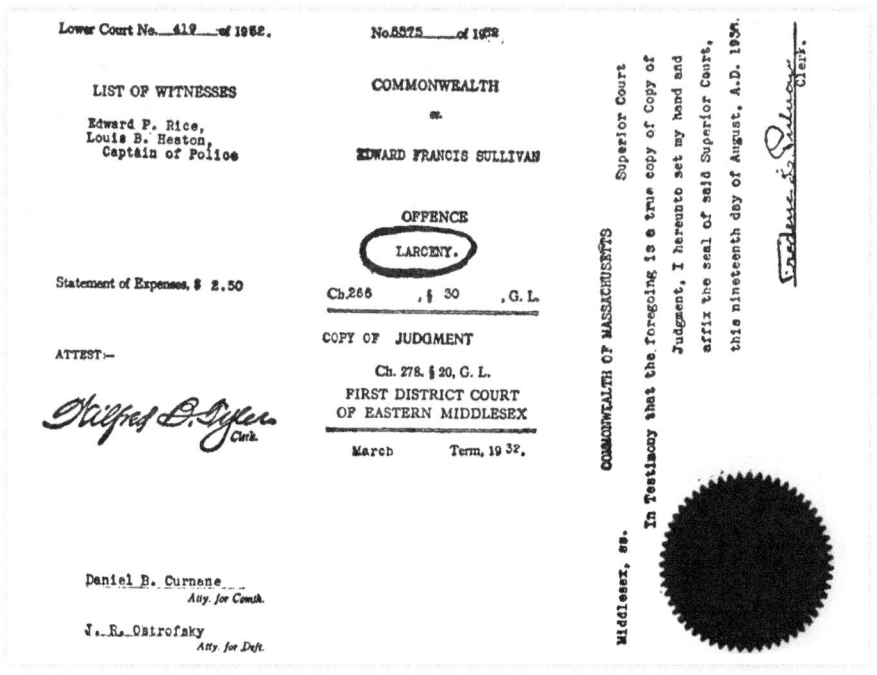

*Reproduction of a document showing that Edward Francis
Sullivan, at one time chief investigator for the Dies Committee,
was convicted of larceny and sentenced to prison.*

World War, instead of going to his home in Sheepshead Bay, drove to the home of Albert Nordenholz at 1572 Castleton Ave., Port Richmond, S. I., where he kept two trunks. Nordenholz, a German-American naturalized citizen for many years, is highly respected by the people in his neighborhood. When Dieckhoff first came to the United States, the Nordenholzes accepted him with open arms. He was the son of an old friend back in Bremerhafen, Germany. Dieckhoff asked permission to keep two trunks in the Nordenholz garret; he stored them there when he went to work in the Brooklyn Navy Yard.

During the two years he worked in the Yard, he would drop around every two weeks or so and go up to the garret to his trunks. Just what he did on those visits, Nordenholz does not know.

On the night Dieckhoff was subpoenaed he suddenly appeared to claim the trunks. He told Nordenholz that he planned to return to Germany. Just what the trunks contained and what he did with them I do not know. They have vanished.

※　※　※

I called upon Dieckhoff in the two-story house in Sheepshead Bay where he lived. He had no intimate friends, didn't smoke, drink or run around. The life of the German war veteran seemed to be confined to working in the Navy Yard, returning home unobtrusively to work on ships' models and making his occasional visits to Nordenholz's garret.

So far as I could learn, Dieckhoff became a marine engineer, working for the North German Lloyd after the World War. In 1923 he entered the United States illegally and remained for two years. Eventually he returned to Germany, but came back to the United States, this time legally, applied for citizenship papers and became a naturalized citizen five years later.

Before he went to work on American war vessels, he worked in various parts of the country—in automobile shops, in the General Electric Co. in Schenectady and as an engineer on Sheepshead Bay boats. Even after Hitler came into power, he worked on Sheepshead Bay boats. After the Berlin-Tokyo axis was formed (1935), Germany became particularly interested in American naval affairs, for the axis, among other things, exchanged military secrets. Shortly before the agreement was made, Dieckhoff suddenly went to work for the Staten Island Shipbuilding Co., Staten Island, which was building four United States destroyers, numbers 364, 365, 384 and 385. He worked on these destroyers during the day. Until late at night he pursued his hobby of building ships' models, which he never made an attempt to sell.

Dieckhoff weighed his words carefully during our talk.

"Why did you apply for a transfer from Staten Island to the Brooklyn Navy Yard?" I asked.

"I don't know," he said. "I guess there was more money in it."

"How much were you getting when you were working on the destroyers?"

"It was some time ago," he said slowly. "I do not remember very good."

"How much are you getting now at the Navy Yard?"

"Forty dollars and twenty-nine cents a week."

"You went to Germany last year for a couple of months and before that you went to Germany for six months. Were you able to save enough for these trips on your wages?"

"I do not spend very much," he said. "I live here all alone."

"How much do you save a week?"

"Oh, I don't know. Ten dollars a week."

"That would make five hundred dollars a year—if you worked steadily, which you didn't. You traveled third class. A round trip would be about two hundred dollars. That would leave you three hundred to spend provided you did not buy clothes, etc., for these trips. How did you manage to live in Germany for six months on three hundred dollars? Did you work there?"

He hesitated and said, "No, I did not work there. I traveled around. I was not in one place."

"How did you do it on three hundred dollars for six months?'

"My brother gave me money."

"What's your brother's business?"

"Oh, just general business in Bremerhafen. He's got a big business there."

"Perhaps I can get a report from the American Consul—"

"Oh," he interrupted. "His business isn't that big."

"Have you a bank account?"

He hesitated again and then said, "No, I do not make enough money for a bank account."

"Where do you keep your money for trips to Germany? In cash?"

"Yes, in cash."

"Where? Here? In this room?"

"No. Not in this room. I have it locked up."

"Where?"

"Oh, different places," he said vaguely.

"Where are those places?"

"I have my money with a friend."

"Who?"

"Nordenholz, Albert Nordenholz."

"You work in Brooklyn, live in Sheepshead Bay and save ten dollars a week in Port Richmond with a friend? Isn't that a long distance to go to save money?"

He shrugged his shoulders without answering.

"What's Nordenholz's business?"

"I think he's retired. I think he used to be a butcher."

"You don't know very much about a man's business and you travel all this distance to give him money to save for you when there are banks all around? Why do you do that?"

"Oh, I don't know. It seems to me that it is better that way."

Later when I asked Nordenholz, he denied that Dieckhoff had ever given him any money to hold.

Dieckhoff had worked on turbines, gear reductions and other complicated mechanical parts on the cruiser "Brooklyn." The moment I asked him if he handled blueprints he answered in the affirmative, but quickly added that the blueprints were returned every night and locked up by the officers. A capable machinist could, he admitted, after careful study remember the blueprints well enough to make a duplicate copy.

"When you went to Germany after working on the destroyers did anyone ever question you about them over there?"

"No," he said quickly. "Nobody."

"My information is that you did talk about structural matters."

He looked startled. "Well," he said, "my brother knew I worked in the Brooklyn Navy Yard. We talked about it, naturally."

"My information is that you talked about it with other people, too."

He stared out of the window with a worried air. Finally he said, "Well, my brother has a friend and I talked with him about it."

"A minute ago you said you had not talked about it with anyone."

"I had forgotten."

"This is the brother who gave you money to travel around in Germany?"

He didn't answer.

"I didn't hear you," I said.

"Yes," Dieckhoff said finally, "he gave me the money."

* * *

I called upon the second of the three suspected spies subpoenaed by the Dies Committee. Alfred Boldt had done very responsible work on the U. S. cruiser "Honolulu." Though he had not been in Germany for ten years, he suddenly got enough money last year to go there and to send his son to school at a Nazi academy. Boldt, too, has no bank account. He needed a minimum of seven hundred dollars for his wife and himself to cross third class, but the Dies Committee was not interested in where the money for the trip had come from.

Boldt left for Germany on August 4, 1936, and returned September 12. On the evening I dropped in to see him, he was tensely nervous. He had heard that someone had been around to talk with Dieckhoff.

"I understand your only son, Helmuth, is going to school in Langin, Germany?" I asked.

"Yes," he said, "I sent him there two years ago."

"No schools in the United States for a fifteen-year-old boy?"

"I wanted him to learn German."

"What do you pay for his schooling over there?"

He hesitated. His wife, who was sitting with us and occasionally advising him in German, suddenly interrupted in German, "Don't tell him. That's German business."

I assume they did not know that I understood, for Boldt passed off her comment as if he had not heard it and said casually, "Oh, twenty-five dollars a month."

"You earn forty dollars a week at the Navy Yard, pay for your son's schooling in Germany, clothes, etc., and you and your wife took more than a month's trip to Germany last year. How do you do it on forty a week?"

His wife giggled a little in the adjoining room. Boldt shrugged his shoulder without answering.

"The cheapest the two of you could do it, third class, would be about seven hundred dollars. Where do you have your bank account?"

"No. No bank account," his wife interrupted sharply.

"All the money is kept here, right here in this house," he laughed.

"You saved all that money in cash?"

"Yes; in cash, right here."

"No banks?"

"We like it better like that—in cash."

Boldt, like Dieckhoff, had been a marine engineer on the North German Lloyd. He went to work in the Brooklyn Navy Yard in 1931. When the cruiser "Honolulu" made its trial run in the spring of 1938, Boldt was on board.

Like Dieckhoff and Boldt, Harry Woulters, *alias* Hugo Woulters, the third of the three subpoenaed men, is a naturalized citizen of German extraction. He went to work in the Navy Yard within one day of Dieckhoff. Before that, both had worked on the same four American destroyers at the Staten Island Shipbuilding Company.

The house where Woulters lives has a great many Jews in it, judging from the names on the letterboxes, and since Hugo sounded too German, he listed his first name as "Harry."

"You and Dieckhoff worked on the same destroyers on Staten Island and you say you never met him there?" I asked.

"No, I never met him until the second day after I went to work in the Navy Yard."

"How many people work on a destroyer—a thousand?"

"Oh, no. Not that many."

"About one hundred?"

"About that," he said uncertainly.

"And you worked with Dieckhoff for six months on the same warships and never met him?"

"Yes," he insisted.

"How come that if you never met him both of you applied for jobs at the Brooklyn Navy Yard at about the same time?"

He shrugged his shoulders. "I don't know. It's funny. Sounds funny, anyway."

"When you worked on the cruiser 'Honolulu' you handled blueprints?"

"Yes, of course, but they were never left in my possession over-night," he added quickly. I couldn't help but think that Dieckhoff, too, had been very quick in protesting that the blueprints had never been left in his possession overnight. They seemed worried about that even though I had not said anything about it.

"Were they *ever* left in your possession overnight?"

"No. They guarded the blueprints—"

"My information is that they were left in your possession."

"Wells, sometimes—blueprints—you know, when you work from blueprints sometimes, yes, sometimes blueprints were left in my pos-session overnight. I was working on reduction gears on the cruiser 'Brooklyn' and I kept the blueprints overnight."

"How often?"

"I can't remember how often. Sometimes the blueprints were kept overnight in my tool box."

"You also worked on turbines and other complicated and confiden-tial structural problems on the warship?"

"Yes."

"And you kept those blueprints overnight, too?"

"Sometimes—not often. Sometimes I left them in my tool box overnight."

Woulters, during the latter period of construction on the "Brooklyn" and the "Honolulu" had got two jobs which most workers do not like. He had the four to midnight and the midnight to eight A.M. watches. Normally Woulters likes to stay at home with his wife.

"While you had these watch duties you had pretty much the run of the ship?"

He hesitated and weighed his words carefully before answering. Finally he nodded and added hastily, "But no one can get on board."

"I didn't ask that. Did you have the run of the ship while everybody else was asleep when you were on watch?"

"Yes," he said in a low voice.

"How did you happen to work in the Brooklyn Navy Yard?"

"Oh, I don't know. I like to work for the Government."

"Have you a bank account?"

"Yes."

"What bank?"

"Oh, I don't know, it's some place on Church Avenue."

"You have about 2,400 dollars in the bank, a nice apartment, and you and your wife went on a trip to Germany last year. Did you save all that money in so short a time on wages of forty dollars a week?"

He shrugged his shoulders.

"Your bank account does not show withdrawals sufficient to cover the trip to Germany—"

"Say," he interrupted excitedly as soon as he saw where the question was leading, "when I was called before the Dies Committee, the Congressman there shook hands with me and asked me if I knew anything about un-American activities in the Navy Yard. I told him I didn't and he told me to go back to work and not to say anything about having been called before them. Now I do not understand why you ask me all these questions. The Congressman told me not to talk and I am saying nothing more. Nothing."

❊　❊　❊

The Dies Congressional Committee was not interested in these three men whom they had subpoenaed and then, oddly enough, refused to question. Besides this very strange procedure by a Committee empowered by the Congress to investigate subversive activities, the Dies Committee withheld for months documentary evidence of Nazi activities in this country directed from Germany. The Committee obtained letters to Guenther Orgell and Peter Gissibl, but quietly placed them in their files without telling anyone about the existence of these documents. They did not subpoena or question the men involved.

The letters the Committee treated so cavalierly are from E. A. Vennekohl in charge of the foreign division of the *Volksbund für das Deutschtum im Ausland* with headquarters in Berlin, letters from the foreign division headquarters in Stuttgart, and from Orgell to Gissibl.

Gissibl was in constant touch with Nazi propaganda headquarters in Germany, receiving instructions and reporting not only on general activities, but especially upon the opening by the Nazis here of schools for children in which Nazi propaganda would be disseminated.

The letters, freely translated, follow. The first is dated October 29, 1937, and was sent by Orgell from his home at Great Kills, S.I.:

Dear Mr. Gissibl:

Many thanks for your prompt reply. My complaint that one cannot get an answer from Chicago refers to the time prior to May, 1937.

I assume from your writing that it is not opportune any more to deliver further books to the *Arbeitsgemeinschaft*, etc.

The material which Mr. Balderman received came from the V.D.A.[21] It has been sent to our Central Book distributing place (Mirbt). If he wishes he can get more any time; that is, if you recommend it.

The thirty books for your Theodore Koerner School, which arrived this summer (via the German Consulate General in Chicago), also came from the V.D.A. If you need more first readers or study books, please write directly to me. Your request then goes immediately—without the official way via the Consulate and Foreign Office—to our Central Book distributing place. Please say how many you need and what else beside

21 Nazi propaganda center for foreign countries with headquarters in Germany.

the first readers and primers[22] you need. I will take care that it will be promptly attended to. Fritz Kuhn, of course, has to be informed of your request and has to give his okay. . . .

With German greetings,

CARL G. ORGELL.

Five days earlier Orgell had written to Gissibl: "You may perhaps remember that I am in charge of the work for the *Volkbund für das Deutschtum im Ausland*[23] for the U.S.A."

Great Kills, 'S.I./NY 24.10.37

Herrn Peter Gissibl
3853/57 North Western Ave.
Chixago, Ill.

Lieber Herr Gissibl;

Sie werden sich vielleicht erinnern, dass ich die VDA (Volksbund fuer das Deutschtum Im Ausland, Berlin) Arbeiten fuer USA erledige.

Unsere Buecherstelle in Berlin moechte nun gerne 2541 Sunnyside Ave. Chicago um Buecher fuer seine "Organisation "(?) gebeten. Kennen Sie ihn ? Welche Organisation leitet er ?

Deutschen Gruss

Carl G. Orgell
Great Kills, S.I./NY

A letter the Dies Committee shelved—Carl G. Orgell identifying himself to Peter Gissibl as a representative of the People's Bund for Germans Living Abroad.

22 The notorious Nazi Primer teaching children songs of hate against Jews and Catholics.

23 People's Bund for Germans Living Abroad.

On March 18, 1938, Gissibl, who had been taking instructions from Orgell, received the following letter from Stuttgart:

Dear Peter:

From your office manager, Comrade Möller, I received a letter dated February 15. He informed me among other things that an exchange of youth is out of the question for this year. I regret this very much. I would like to see, in the interests of our common efforts, if we would have had youth all ready this year, especially also from your district. Perhaps it is still possible with your support. The time, of course, which is still at our disposal, is very limited. This I can see clearly.

I will write to you again in greater detail soon. In the meantime you can perhaps send me more detailed information about the development of your school during the past weeks; I recommend again the fulfillment of your justified wishes wholeheartedly. Let us hope that the result might be achieved very soon towards which we in common strive.

Hearty greetings from house to house.

In loyal comradeship,

Yours,

G. MOSHACK.

On May 20, 1938, E. A. Vennekohl, of the People's Bund for Germans Living Abroad, wrote to Gissibl as follows:

Dear Comrade Gissibl:

We wrote you yesterday that the 3,000 badges for the singing festival would be sent to you via Orgell; for various reasons we have now divided the badges in ten single packages of which

Deutsches Ausland-Institut Stuttgart

Fernsprecher 26257-26259 + Telegramm: Auslandinstitut + Postscheckkonto: Stuttgart 840
Bankverbindung: Deutsche Bank und Diskonto Gesellschaft, Abt. Gymnasiumstr. Stuttgart

Haus des Deutschtums

Unser Zeichen: AV - KB/Wi.   Stuttgart-S, den 18. März 1938

Herrn
Peter Gissibl
Amerika-Deutscher Volksbund
3855 N.Western Avenue

C h i c a g o , Ill.
U.S.A.

Lieber Peter!

Von Deinem Amtsträger, dem Kameraden Möller, erhielt ich unter
dem 15. Februar ein Schreiben. Er teilte mir u.a. mit, dass
ein Austausch von Jugendlichen für dieses Jahr nicht mehr in
Frage kommt. Ich bedauere das sehr. Ich hätte es im Interesse
unserer gemeinsamen Bestrebungen sehr gerne gesehen, wenn wir
bereits in diesem Jahre, gerade auch aus Eurem Kreise, Jugendliche
hier gehabt hätten. Vielleicht lässt sich mit Deiner Unter-
stützung diese Möglichkeit doch noch schaffen. Die Zeit, die
noch zur Verfügung steht, ist allerdings sehr knapp bemessen.
Darüber bin ich mir durchaus im klaren.

Ich werde Dir demnächst wieder ausführlicher schreiben. In der
Zwischenzeit kannst Du mir vielleicht nähere Angaben über die
Entwicklung Deiner Schule während der letzten Wochen übermitteln.
Eine Erfüllung Deiner berechtigten Wünsche habe ich erneut aufs
wärmste befürwortet. Hoffentlich lässt sich auch sehr bald das
Ergebnis erzielen, um das wir gemeinsam bestrebt sind.

Herzliche Grüsse von Haus zu Haus
                              in treuer Kameradschaft

                              Dein G. Wohlach

Another letter connecting Gissibl with a German propaganda agency.
This letter, translated in the text, was hardly noticed by the Dies Committee.

two each went to the following addresses: Friedrich Schlenz, Karl Moeller, Karl Kraenzle, Orgell and two to you.

Please inform your co-workers respectively and take care that in case duties have to be paid they should be laid out; please see to it that Orgell refunds the money to you later; this was the simplest and the only way by which the badges could be sent in order to arrive on time.

With the German people's greetings,

E. A. VENNEKOHL.

These documents in the hands of the Dies Committee show definite tie-ups between German propaganda divisions and agents in the United States (some of them came through the Nazi diplomatic corps), yet these documents were put aside. The letters from True, Allen, and others quoted in the previous chapter were also placed before the Congressional Committee. It refused to call the men involved.

Volksbund für das Deutschtum im Ausland
Hauptgeschäftsstelle

Bankkonten: Deutsche ·Bank, Depositenkasse C 3, Berlin W 62, Kleiststr. 22; Bank der Deutschen Arbeit, Berlin SW 19, Wallstr. 61–65. Postscheckkonto: Berlin NW 7, Nr. 84 67. Drahtanschrift: Deutschtum Berlin.

Unser Zeichen: Vel/Gr.　　　　　Ihr Zeichen:　　　　　Berlin W 30, den 20. Mai 1938
In der Antwort anzugeben.　　　　　　　　　　　　　　Martin-Luther-Str. 97
　　　　　　　　　　　　　　　　　　　　　　　　　Fernruf 25 91 55

Betrifft:

　　　　Herrn
　　　　Peter Gissibl
　　　　3855 North Western Ave.
　　　　Chicago, Ill.
　　　　U.S.A.

Lieber Kamerad Gissibl!

Wir schrieben Ihnen gestern, dass die 3.000 Sängerfestplaketten
über Orgell an Sie geleitet würden. Aus verschiedenen Gründen
haben wir die Plaketten jetzt in zehn Einzelpakete verteilt,
von denen je zwei anfolgende Anschriften gingen:
Friedrich Schlenz, Karl Moeller, Karl Kraenzle, Orgell und zwei an
Sie.
Bitte informieren Sie Ihre Mitarbeiter entsprechend und tragen
Sie Sorge, dass die etwaigen Zollspesen verauslagt werden. Diese
wollen Sie sich später von Herrn Orgell zurückvergüten lassen.
Es war dies der einfachste und einzigste Weg, auf dem die Plaketten
versandt werden konnten, um rechtzeitig drüben einzutreffen.

　　　　　　　　　　Mit volksdeutschem Gruss
　　i.A.

　　　　　　　E.A. Vennekohl

Further evidence of Gissibl's tie-up with the People's Bund for Germans Living Abroad. This letter, a translation of which appears in the text, was also long withheld by the Dies Committee.

CONCLUSION

THE ACTIVITIES OF THE FEW agents and propagandists described in the foregoing chapters do not, as I said in the preface, even scratch the surface of what seem to be widespread efforts to interfere in the internal affairs of the American people and their Government; but a few basic conclusions can reasonably be drawn from what little is known of the Fifth Column's operations.

Berlin-directed agents in foreign countries sometimes combine propaganda and espionage, frequently using the propaganda organizations as the bases for espionage. In the United States, so far as I have been able to ascertain, agents of the Rome-Berlin-Tokyo axis are just beginning to cooperate. In the Central and South American countries, however, the axis has apparently agreed to a division of labor, each of the fascist powers assuming a specific field of activity.

Germany, Italy and Japan have already shown the extent to which they will go in their drive for raw materials vital to their industries and war machines. In Spain, the German and Italian Fifth Column organized and fomented a bloody civil war in order to establish a wide fascist area to the south of France, for Germany and Italy, of course, consider France a potential enemy in the next war. In France itself, German and Italian agents, aided by their Governments, built an amazing network of steel and concrete fortifications manned by at least 100,000 heavily armed men—all this before France awoke to the treason within her own borders.

The strategy pursued by the Fifth Column in different countries falls into like patterns. In Austria, before it was swallowed, Nazi agents first established propaganda organizations as the bases from which to work. When, after the abortive attempt to seize the Austrian Government, the Nazis were made illegal, they went underground but continued to get aid from Germany. Eventually Berlin ordered *Standarte II* organized as a specific body prepared to provoke disturbances. When the Austrian police quelled them, the provocations enabled Germany to protest that German citizens were being attacked and mistreated. The activities of *Standarte II,* directed by the Gestapo, continued with increasing intensity until the unfortunate country was absorbed.

In Czechoslovakia the same strategy was followed: first the establishment of propaganda centers to which Nazis and Nazi sympathizers could gravitate—under the cloak of bodies seeking to improve relations between the Sudeten Germans and the Czech Government; then the utilization of propaganda headquarters and branches as centers for espionage. Shortly before the Munich Pact, *Standarte II* again came into being, creating disorders which, when Czech police tried to suppress them, enabled Germany to raise the cry that Czech subjects of German blood were being cruelly mistreated.

Invariably the aggressor nation raises a moral issue to cover up proposed acts of aggression. Italy wanted to "civilize the Ethiopians" by dropping bombs on defenseless women and children. Germany and Italy openly sent aid to Franco "to keep Spain from being Bolshevized." And so on. The broad "moral issue" on the international field to cover up aggressions by the Rome-Berlin-Tokyo axis is "Communism." The axis, announced as having been formed "to exchange information about Communism," is really a military alliance now generally recognized.

With the same issue, the axis is now boring into the Western Hemisphere. Actually the reasons seem to be military and not missionary.

Germany, especially, has sent and is sending agents not only to carry on espionage but to organize groups for political pressure upon the American republics. I very much doubt, from all I have been able to learn, if the motive is primarily to win the Americas over to the joys of totalitarian government or to the theory of Aryan supremacy. The money and the effort seem to be expended for more practical reasons. The Bunds can exert not only political pressure, but can develop natives with fascist leanings into the spies and *saboteurs* so badly needed in war time; for this reason it is worth the enormous effort and money it is costing the aggressor nations.

When the long expected war breaks, neither Europe nor the Far East will be in a condition to supply war materials and foodstuffs to the warring countries. The chief sources of raw materials will be the Western Hemisphere. A strong foothold in the Americas means a tremendous advantage in the coming struggle, since materials are as important to an army as is man power. And, should the fascist powers be unable to get these raw materials for themselves, secret agents can at least sabotage shipments to enemy countries—as did German agents in the United States during the first years of the World War, while we were still neutral.

Mexico, because of its enormous oil supplies, plays an important part in fascist military strategy. Consequently, we find intensive efforts by the axis, and especially Germany, to overthrow the Cárdenas Government because it is avowedly antifascist. A fascist government, helped into power by the Rome-Berlin-Tokyo axis, could be depended upon to supply much needed oil in war time.

The United States, as one of the world's greatest sources of raw materials and foodstuffs, is an even more important factor. Germany has not forgotten that its armies had the Allies on their knees when American supplies and American man power turned their imminent victory into defeat; should America be on the side of the democracies as against the fascist powers, sabotaging shipments of supplies and men will be as important as crushing an enemy line.

The tactics utilized in the Western Hemisphere by the Fifth Column are similar to those used in Europe. Propaganda machines, masquerading as organizations designed to promote better relationships between a fascist and an American nation, are set up. Fascist movements are organized, usually from across national boundaries. In Mexico, Nazi agents operating out of the United States organized the Gold Shirts; subsequently, as in Austria, a Putsch was attempted (in 1935 and again in 1938). The storing of arms in Sonora by General Yocupicio, who is working with Nazi agents, promises another rebellion when the time seems ripe.

In Central America, the axis is presenting small republics with gifts of arms in efforts to win their friendship. Agents sent from Germany are establishing Nazi centers and the home Government is supplying them with propaganda. In Panama the situation is somewhat more sharp. There Japan has always had an intense interest in the Canal. In the axis, Germany has become a co-worker since she has large colonies in Brazil and Colombia, next door to the Panama Canal. These colonies are now being organized at a feverish pace while the countries themselves are deluged with propaganda over special short-wave beams. In Brazil, a Nazi-directed abortive Putsch took place in 1938.

These activities point to an objective which certainly is not calculated to be in the interest of the United States and our Monroe Doctrine. From all indications the efforts appear directed toward ringing the United States with fascist countries, or at least countries with fascist bodies capable of giving the United States a headache should she ever be involved in a war with one or all of the axis powers.

In the United States itself we find that the strategy is the same as that followed in Austria, Czechoslovakia and in countries of the Western World. The German-American Bund functions "to promote better relations between the United States and Germany," but the efforts consist of persistent anti-American and anti-democratic propaganda and, within the past year or two, of serving as a base for military and naval spies.

With Germany directing the strategy, her agents in all countries raise the issue of the "menace of the Jew and the Catholic," with especial emphasis upon the Jew; the Catholics are still too strong for the Nazis to come to grips with at this time.

The Federal Government, of course, has ample legal machinery for prosecuting spies, but espionage is only part of the broad Nazi campaign against this democratic Government. So far as the Western World is concerned, the Federal Government has already taken steps to try to counteract the short-wave broadcasts by German and Italian government-controlled stations. Counter broadcasts are being employed as a defensive measure, and though of value, will probably not completely counteract fascist "news" agencies supplying propaganda in the guise of news, free of charge, to the Central and South American newspapers as well as printed propaganda sent from Germany and distributed by the bunds. Outside of military action, economic pressure seems to be the only language the fascist governments understand, and a little of that pressure by the American Government would probably make them understand our resentment at their invasion far more than broadcasts and general talk about a family of nations in the Western Hemisphere.

Our laws and courts provide a machinery which can be used to prevent any infringement upon the democratically constituted rights of the people. It is of vital importance, however, that preparations for fascist lawlessness be vigilantly uprooted. The Italian and German people made just this fatal mistake of tolerating the activities of Mussolini's and Hitler's gangs until they grew strong enough to seize power and crush every sign of democracy.

There is no reason why a great people, attacked by a pernicious ideology, cannot counteract such propaganda with greater and more intelligent propaganda to educate our people to the advantages of democracy—to what fascism really means to everyone, including the big industrialists and financiers, some of whom have been flirting with fascism. The Government, however, can and should be instructed by the representatives of the people, to take proper steps to stop the infiltration of Nazi agents and propagandists into this country.

There are various other and perhaps more practical and useful steps which can be taken, but those can be worked out once the people awake to the danger of permitting fascist propaganda to go on, and sentiment becomes strong enough to put an end to foreign-directed activities here.

— THE END —